C Language
for Programmers

Kenneth Pugh

Pugh-Killeen Associates

Scott, Foresman and Company
Glenview, Illinois • London

1 2 3 4 5 6 – KPF – 89 88 87 86 85 84

ISBN 0-673-18034-4

Copyright © 1985 Scott, Foresman and Company.

All Rights Reserved.

Printed in the United States of America.

Library of Congress Cataloging in Publication Data

Pugh, Kenneth.
  C language for programmers.

  Includes index.
  1. C (Computer program language) I. Title.
QA76.73.C15P84   1984   001.64′24   84-20263
ISBN 0-673-18034-4

CP/M and CP/M-86 are trademarks of Digital Research.
MS-DOS is a trademark of Microsoft.
APPLE is a trademark of Apple Computers, Inc.
UNIX is a trademark of Bell Laboratories.

Preface

C is a language rapidly gaining in popularity among programmers. The language is quite portable; that is, programs written in C can run on a variety of machines without significant alterations. The portability is due to the conciseness of the language and the absence of significant variations in compilers. The portability of C and its speed, which can approach that of assembly language, make it an ideal choice for many applications. Although originally designed for the UNIX operating system, C has spread to many popular microcomputer systems, such as CP/M, CP/M-86, MS-DOS, and APPLE-DOS.

The design of C allows the construction of many statements that appear quite foreign to programmers in other languages. This book was developed to ease the transition from BASIC, FORTRAN, PL/I, COBOL, and PASCAL to C. It is assumed that the reader has some programming background in one of these languages or a similar type of language. The reader who knows only interpreted BASIC is advised to read Appendixes I and J, which give some concepts of compiled languages. Appendix H has some introductory material on bits, bytes, and numbers. Each programming concept in the book has a flowchart associated with it, so that it can be understood without reference to these languages.

The C language has a de facto reference standard, Appendix A of *The C Programming Language* by Brian W. Kernighan and Dennis M. Ritchie. Most commercially available compilers use that standard or reference it as to their deficiencies or differences. The usual deficiency in compilers is the absence of bit fields and floating variables and operations. Some compilers have slight differences, mostly in the areas of external variables, nesting of comments, and number of significant characters in variable names. The reader is advised to consult his compiler's manual for explanations of how it may differ from the standard.

The C compiler on the UNIX Version 7 operating system has a few additions to the language that are not in the Kernighan and Ritchie standard. These are enumerated variables, the void data type for functions, and the ability for structures to be assigned and to be passed and returned from functions. These are found in some compilers other than the UNIX compiler and are noted in the text as UNIX compiler features. Currently, C language is undergoing a formal standardization effort by the American National Standards Institute (ANSI).

The other languages have their own dialects, even those that have been standardized. In creating samples from other languages, I selected the dialects with the fewest extensions. The BASIC was APPLESOFT. Due to the popularity of the BASIC from Microsoft, extensions of that dialect over APPLESOFT are shown separately. The FORTRAN is FORTRAN-66. FORTRAN-77 has several more features that have equivalents in C. The reader who is familiar with the latter FORTRAN should have no difficulty in picking these out. PASCAL is PASCAL without the UCSD extensions. COBOL is the ANSI standard. PL/I is the IBM standard.

Kenneth Pugh

Dedication

This book is dedicated to Leslie Killeen, my wife, who endured the many hours of computer talk, and to Nameless, our cat, who sat on my arm as I composed it at the terminal.

My appreciation to Jose Abeyta, Ajay Agrwawal, Allan Ames, David Carroll, David Crocker, John DeBossu, Joe DeStefano, Thomas Dressing, Eric Johnson, Tom McLaren, Glenn Meader, Win Piper, Alan Robinson, Richard Walton, and John Yates for reviewing the manuscript and providing helpful comments; to countless others for a comment here and a correction there; and to Richard Staron, my editor at Scott, Foresman & Company, who got me started with this book.

Contents

1

Introduction

C is a procedure-oriented language. Parts of its composition resemble that of other procedure-oriented languages, such as BASIC and FORTRAN. It has all the constructs associated with "structured programming"—the *if-then-else,* the *while,* and the *case.* It also includes features such as pointers, which allow access to many machine-language capabilities without having to use assembly language.

SAMPLE PROGRAM

The best introduction to C is a program. Flowchart 1.1 describes a simple program that determines which of two input numbers is larger and then multiplies it by 2. The program in C may look like:

```
main ()
/* Outputs twice the larger number entered */
  {
  float numone,numtwo,outnum;
  printf("Enter two numbers ");
  scanf("%f%f",&numone,&numtwo);
  if (numone>numtwo)
    outnum = numone*2.;
    else
    outnum = numtwo*2.;
  printf("Double the largest number is %f",outnum);
  exit (0);
  }
```

The first line of the program **main** ( ) states that it is the first or main routine to be executed. Routines are described in Chapter 4. The next line is a comment and is ignored by the compiler. The left brace ({) on the third line begins the body of the program. The body includes the declaration of variables followed by executable statements. The following line declares the three variables that will be used in the routine. Declarations are covered in Chapter 2. Function **printf** prints the characters in quotes on the terminal. Function **scanf** inputs two values from the terminal keyboard. The **%f** tells **scanf** that numbers are to be input. These two functions are covered in Chapter 8.

The next four lines calculate the value of **outnum** in one of two ways, depending on the comparison of **numone** and **numtwo**. The if-else is described in Chapter 3. The second **printf** prints the value of **outnum**

1

Flowchart 1.1 SAMPLE DOUBLE NUMBER PROGRAM

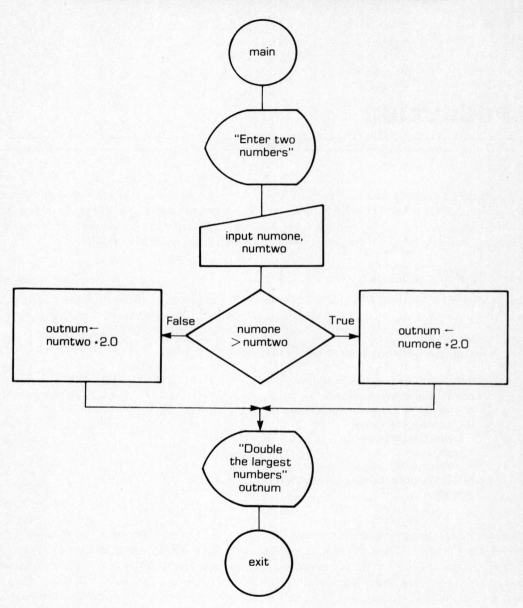

on the terminal. **exit (0)** terminates the execution of the program. The right brace (}) on the last line ends the body of the program.

The process of compiling and linking this program to make it executable is described in Appendix J.

For comparison, the program is shown in other languages in Exhibit 1.1. Note that the actual operation of each program is slightly different, especially in the input or output operations. As shown, the FORTRAN and COBOL programs require that the input numbers appear in certain columns in the input. The other programs have a free form input. That is, one can introduce any number of spaces between the two numbers, and the program will ignore them. With the above format for **scanf**, any number of spaces (but no comma) can be entered between the two numbers that are input. A more detailed explanation of input and output using **scanf** and **printf** appears in Chapter 8.

The style of the program is similar to other languages, but the program is not an optimal one. The conversant C programmer might write it as:

```
main ( )
/* Outputs twice the larger number entered */
  {
  float numone,numtwo;
  printf ("Enter two numbers ");
  scanf ("%f%f",&numone,&numtwo);
  printf ("\nDouble the largest number is %f",
     (numone>numtwo ? numone*2. : numtwo*2.) );
  exit (0);
  }
```

This appears slightly less comprehensible than the first version, but it will execute faster. In most examples in this book, both a C version that appears similar to other languages and a more compact C version are given.

As noted in the introduction, the dialects of the languages used in the examples are those with the fewest features. BASIC and FORTRAN programmers will note especially that the more advanced versions of these languages would look much more like the C version. For devotees of other languages, the COBOL program may look a bit complex. A large portion of it is required code that is proportionally smaller in larger programs.

Typestyle

Throughout this book, the common capitalization will be used for commands and variables. C is a case-sensitive language and requires that all keywords be in lower case. Variables are shown lower case. Macros (**#defines**) are shown upper case. Programs in other languages will be shown in upper case.

TYPICAL COMPUTER

The C language is highly portable. There are compilers that run on computers from the size of an IBM 370 to a DEC PDP-11 to an IBM-PC, which uses an Intel 8088 microprocessor, to an 8-bit Apple, which uses an MOS technology 6502 microprocessor. A program written in C for one machine will work on another machine with minor changes, mostly in the input and output interfacing (such as file names).

Exhibit 1.1 SAMPLE PROGRAM IN OTHER LANGUAGES

BASIC

```
  5 REM OUTPUTS TWICE THE LARGER NUMBER
10 PRINT "ENTER TWO NUMBERS"
20 INPUT N1,N2
30 IF N1>N2 THEN OU=N1*2 : GOTO 50
40 OU=N2*2
50 PRINT "DOUBLE THE LARGEST NUMBER IS",OU
60 END
```

MBASIC

```
  5 REM OUTPUTS TWICE THE LARGER NUMBER
10 PRINT "ENTER TWO NUMBERS"
20 INPUT N1, N2
30 IF N1>N2 THEN OU=N1*2 ELSE OU=N2*2
40 PRINT "DOUBLE THE LARGEST NUMBER IS", OU
50 END
```

FORTRAN

```
C     OUTPUTS TWICE THE LARGER NUMBER
      REAL NUMONE,NUMTWO,
      WRITE(6,50)
50    FORMAT(17HENTER TWO NUMBERS)
      READ (5,100) NUMONE,NUMTWO
100 FORMAT(F10.3,F10.3)
      IF (NUMONE.GT.NUMTWO) GOTO 200
      NUMOUT=NUMTWO*2
      GOTO 300
200 NUMOUT=NUMONE*2
300 WRITE(6,400) NUMOUT)
400 FORMAT(30HDOUBLE THE LARGEST NUMBER IS ,F10.3)
      END
```

PASCAL

```
PROGRAM DOUNUM(INPUT,OUTPUT);
(* OUTPUTS TWICE THE LARGER NUMBER *)
VAR:
   NUMONE,NUMTWO,NUMOUT : REAL;
BEGIN
   WRITE('ENTER TWO NUMBERS');
   READ(NUMONE,NUMTWO);
   IF (NUMONE>NUMTWO) THEN
      NUMOUT:=NUMONE*2
   ELSE
      NUMOUT:=NUMTWO*2;
   WRITE('DOUBLE THE LARGEST NUMBER IS',NUMOUT);
END.
```

PL/I

```
PROCEDURE OPTIONS(MAIN);
/* OUTPUTS TWICE THE LARGER NUMBER */
DECLARE NUMONE,NUMTWO FLOAT;
```

Exhibit 1.1 SAMPLE PROGRAM IN OTHER LANGUAGES (continued)

```
PUT LIST ('ENTER TWO NUMBERS');
GET LIST (NUMONE, NUMTWO);
   IF (NUMONE>NUMTWO) THEN
   NUMOUT = NUMONE*2;
ELSE
   NUMOUT = NUMTWO*2;
PUT LIST ('DOUBLE THE LARGEST NUMBER IS', NUMOUT);
END;
```

COBOL

```
IDENTIFICATION DIVISION.
PROGRAM-ID.
   DOUNUM.
REMARKS.
   OUTPUTS TWICE THE LARGER NUMBER.
ENVIRONMENT DIVISION.
INPUT-OUTPUT SECTION.
FILE-CONTROL.
   SELECT PRINT-FILE ASSIGN TO OUTPUT.
   SELECT READ-FILE ASSIGN TO INPUT.
DATA DIVISION.
FILE SECTION.
FD   PRINT-FILE
      LABEL RECORDS ARE OMITTED.
01   PRINT-LINE PICTURE X (80).
FD   READ-FILE
      LABEL RECORDS ARE OMITTED.
01   IN-REC.
      02 NUMONE   PICTURE 9999999V999.
      02 NUMTWO   PICTURE 9999999V999.
WORKING-STORAGE SECTION.
01   ASK-LINE
      02 FILLER PICTURE X (17) VALUE "ENTER TWO NUMBERS"
01   OUT-LINE.
      02 FILLER PICTURE X(30) VALUE "DOUBLE THE LARGEST NUMBER IS"
      02 NUMOUT PICTURE 999999.999.
PROCEDURE DIVISION.
   OPEN INPUT READ-FILE
      OUTPUT PRINT-FILE.
   WRITE PRINT-LINE FROM ASK-LINE.
   READ READ-FILE.
   IF NUMONE IS GREATER THAN NUMTWO
      COMPUTE NUMOUT = NUMONE*2.
   ELSE
      COMPUTE NUMOUT = NUMTWO*2.
   WRITE PRINT-LINE FROM OUT-LINE.
   CLOSE READ-FILE PRINT-FILE.
   STOP RUN.
```

To reference examples in this book to the memory of a computer, a typical processor has been used. It has the following characteristics:

Object Type	Size
Byte	8 bits
Character	1 byte
Integer	2 bytes
Float	4 bytes

Where a memory diagram is given, the addresses are in decimal format.

2

Variables and Operators

The simple variable and constant types in C can be found in most other languages. However, C has several more operators than most languages. Many of these additional operators, such as the bitwise shifts and the prefix and postfix increment and decrement, can take advantage of specific machine features that other languages do not use.

VARIABLES

C supports most of the common data types for variables—integer, real (float), and character. In addition, there are a few variations on the integer type—short, long, and unsigned—and a long float (double). All variables must be declared before their use. A declaration is of the form:

type variable-name;

or

type variable-name, variable-name . . . ;

where *type* is a type of variable and the *variable–names* are separated by commas. Types of variables include **int** (integer), **char** (character), **float** (floating point) and **double** (double precision floating point). Variable names must begin with a letter or underscore('A' to 'Z', 'a' to 'z', and '_'). The rest of the name can be letters, underscore, or digits. Only the first eight characters are significant on most compilers. If no type is given, it defaults to **int**. Examples of declarations are:

int i;	declares **i** to be an integer variable
int j,k;	declares **j** and **k** to be integer variables
char c;	declares **c** to be a character variable
float f;	declares **f** to be a float (real) variable
double d;	declares **d** to be a long float (double) variable

The corresponding declarations in other languages are shown in Exhibit 2.1.

Three variations of the integer type are supported. The **short** integer is either shorter or the same length as a regular integer, depending on the computer. It is used to save space when many integer variables are

Exhibit 2.1 VARIABLE DECLARATIONS IN OTHER LANGUAGES

BASIC

I%	integer:
C$	character:
F	float:
D#	double:

(these are derived from the suffix on the name of the variable)

FORTRAN

INTEGER I	integer
REAL F	float
DOUBLE D	double

(no character in FORTRAN-66)

PASCAL

I : INTEGER;	integer
C : CHAR;	character
F : REAL;	float

(no double in PASCAL)

PL/I

DECLARE I FIXED BINARY (15,0);	integer
DECLARE C CHAR(1);	character
DECLARE F FLOAT BINARY(31);	float
DECLARE D FLOAT BINARY(63);	double

COBOL

02 I PICTURE 99999.	integer
02 C PICTURE X.	character
02 F PICTURE 9999V999.	float
02 D PICTURE 999999999999V999.	double[3]

required. The **long** integer is either the same length or longer than the regular integer. It is used to hold larger numbers than a regular integer. The **unsigned** integer variable contains only positive values. That is, the most significant bit is not used for the sign. (See Appendix H for more explanation of signed values.)

long int i;	declares **i** to be a long integer variable
short int j;	declares **i** to be a short integer variable
unsigned int i;	declares **i** to be an unsigned integer variable

The UNIX compiler supports a variable type called the **unsigned char**. This character is the same size as **char**, but the most significant bit is not treated as a sign bit when it is converted to an integer. (See the section in this chapter on the conversions.)

Size of variables

For the typical computer and compiler, the sizes of these types are:

Variable Type	Size	Range
char	1 byte	−128 to 127 or 0 to 255, depending on compiler
int	2 bytes	−32768 to 32767
float	4 bytes	-1.7×10^{38} to 1.7×10^{38} (6 digit precision)
double	8 bytes	-1.7×10^{38} to 1.7×10^{38} (16 digit precision)
short int	2 bytes	−32768 to 32767
long int	4 bytes	−2147483648 to 2147483647
unsigned int	2 bytes	0 to 65535

CONSTANTS

There are several types of constants—integer, float, character, and string. These correspond to the constants in most other languages.

Numeric constants

Numeric constants include integers, octal and hexidecimal constants, longs, and floats. Octal and hexadecimal constants are integer constants that are expressed in their respective bases. Octal constants are preceded by a zero (**0**). Hexadecimal constants are preceded by a leading **0X** or **0x**. Integer constants may be explicitly defined as long in most compilers (i.e., the same size as a **long** variable) by adding a suffix of **L** or **l**. If the value is greater than can be held in the size of an **int**, then the compiler makes it **long**. Float constants are always stored as the same length as **double** variables. Exhibit 2.2 lists the equivalents of these C constants in other languages.

Numeric Constant	Meaning
32	integer constant
034	octal constant
0XFE,0xFD	hexadecimal constants
32.3,12.5E-7	float constant
32L	long constant
567893	long constant (implicit)

Character constants

Character constants equal the numeric equivalent of the bit configuration by which a particular character is represented in a machine. Most machines use either ASCII (American Standard for Information Interchange) or EBCDIC (Extended Binary Coded Decimal Interchange Code). To ensure portability, character constants should be used rather than the integer equivalents. Character constants are denoted by a character enclosed in single quotes.

Character Constant	ASCII Value
'A'	65
'Z'	90
'='	61

Exhibit 2.2 CONSTANTS IN OTHER LANGUAGES

BASIC

32	integer constant
32.3, 12.5E-7	float constants
"A"	single character constant
"ABCDEF"	string constant

FORTRAN

32	integer constant
32.3, 12.5E-7	float constants
1HA	character constant in data statement
6HABCDEF	character constants in data statement

PASCAL

32	integer constant
32.3, 12.5E-7	float constants
'A'	single character constant
'ABCDEF'	string constant

PL/I

32	integer constant
32.3, 12.5E-7	float constants
'011100'B	octal constant represented by binary constant
'11111110'B	hexadecimal constant represented by binary constant
'A'	single character constant
'ABCDE'	string constant

COBOL

32	integer constant
32.3, 12.5E-7	float constants
"A"	single character constant
"ABCDE"	string constant

Escape sequences represent non-printable characters and characters that have meaning in the C language. An escape sequence consists of the escape character (the backslash '\') and a second character.

Escape Sequence	Character Represented
'\n'	newline character (LF)
'\t'	tab character (HT)
'\\'	backslash character
'\''	single quote
'\0'	null character
'\b'	backspace character (BS)
'\f'	formfeed character (FF)
'\r'	carriage return character (CR)
'\"'	double quote

Any **char**-sized pattern can be represented by the escape character followed by one to three octal digits. This is used mainly to represent a non-printable character for which there is no escape sequence. For example:

Character	Value	ASCII
'\017'	decimal 15	SI
'\4'	decimal 4	EOT

A string constant is stored in memory as a collection of character constants terminated by a special character (the null character '\0'). The string is surrounded by double quotes rather than the single quotes used to surround a character constant. Strings are discussed in Chapter 5. The escape sequences for characters can be used in a string.

Constant	Meaning
"ABCDE"	string constant consisting of the characters 'A', 'B', 'C', 'D', 'E' and \0'
" "	string constant consisting of \0'

Exhibit 2.2 lists the equivalents of the character and string constants in other languages.

INITIALIZATION

Initialization of variables is optional at the time of declaration. If not initialized, the value of a variable may be either 0 or garbage, depending on the storage class of the variable (see the section in this chapter on storage classes). To initialize a variable in a declaration, follow the variable name by an equal sign (=) and the value. For example:

int i=5;	declares **i** to be an integer with initial value of 5
float f=32.5;	declares **f** to be a floating number with initial value of 32.5
char c='A';	declares **c** to be a character variable with an initial value of the machine representation of the character **A**

STORAGE CLASSES

There are four storage classes in C—automatic, static, register, and external. (External storage is discussed in Chapter 4.)

auto

The memory locations for automatic variables—**auto**—are allocated when a routine is entered. When the routine completes, the locations are returned for re-use by other routines. By default, every variable declared inside a routine is assumed to be **auto**, unless the declaration explicitly specifies otherwise. If an **auto** variable is initialized in the declaration statement, then every time a routine is entered, it is reinitialized to that value. Otherwise it is garbage. Any valid expression may be used to initialize an **auto** variable.

static

The memory locations for the variables with storage class **static** are set aside at compile time and do not change as the program executes. The initialization for a **static** variable takes place at compile time. If a **static** variable is not explicitly initialized, its value is 0.

register

A **register** variable acts like an **auto** variable. The register designation tells the compiler to use a machine register instead of a memory location for the variable. If a variable is used frequently in a routine, it speeds up the code on most machines. If the number of variables designated as **register** in a routine exceeds the number of machine registers, the excess are treated as **auto** variables.

EXPRESSIONS

An expression in C is simply a combination of variables, function calls, and constants connected together by operators whose evaluation yields a value. Many expressions in C look exactly like those in other languages. There are, however, a few rules that are covered in the next sections on how expressions are evaluated.

OPERATORS

C has several operators that act the same as those in other lanaguages. These include arithmetic, relational, logical, and bitwise. The postfix, prefix, assignment, and conditional operators are unique to C.

Arithmetic

Arithmetic operators are the standard add, subtract, multiply, and divide. These are represented by +, −, *, and /. If the types of the values on either side of the operator are different, one will be converted to the type of the other. The rules for this conversion are discussed later in this chapter. Examples of expressions with arithmetic operators include:

Expression	Has the Value
5+i	5 added to the value of the variable **i**
22.3∗f	22.3 multiplied by the value of the variable **f**
k/3	the value of variable **k** divided by 3
x−y	the value of the variable **x** less the value of the variable **y**

The result of an integer divided by an integer is the truncated whole number. The remainder of an integer division is given by the modulus operator %. Thus:

Expression	Has the Value
22/3	7
22%3	1

There is also a unary − (i.e., the minus sign). There is no exponentiation operator, unlike in most other languages.

Relational operators

C provides relational operators much like those in other languages. They are == (equal to), != (not equal to), > (greater than), < (less than), >= (greater than or equal to), and <= (less than or equal to). The result of two values connected by a relational operator is either the value 0 for false or 1 for true. Thus:

Expression	Has the Value
5<3	0
3<5	1
5==5	1
3==5	0
i<=3	0 if the variable **i** is greater than 3, 1 otherwise

Unlike many other languages, there is no logical variable type in C. Any value can be tested for true or false. If the value is nonzero, it is true. If it is zero, it is false. This is further described in Chapter 3.

Logical operators

The two logical binary operators are **&&** (and) and **||** (inclusive or). The result of their operation is either a 0 (false) or 1 (true). Unlike the other operators, they are always evaluated from left to right. For **&&**, if the left expression is 0, the right expression is not evaluated. For **||**, if the left expression is nonzero, then the right expression is not evaluated. This is summarized as follows:

&& (AND)

Left Expression	Right Expression	Value of Result
0	not evaluated	0
non-zero	0	0
non-zero	non-zero	1

|| (OR)

Left Expression	Right Expression	Value of Result
0	0	0
0	non-zero	1
non-zero	not evaluated	1

For example:

Expression	Has the Value
5 || 3	1
5 || 0	1
5 && 3	1
5 && 0	0
i || j	0 if both **i** and **j** contain 0, 1 otherwise

The negation operator (!) reverses the sense of the value following it. A non-zero value is converted to a 0 and a zero value is converted to a 1.

Expression	Has the Value
!5	0
!0	1
!i	0 if **i** is non-zero, 1 if **i** is 0

Bitwise operators

Several bitwise operators are available in C. These operate only on integers. The operators include **&** (and), **|** (or), **∧** (exclusive-or), **<<** (left shift), **>>** (right shift), and the unary **~** (one's complement). These are usually used to turn bits on or off or to test specific bits in integer or character variables. The left shift operation fills the rightmost bits with 0s. The right shift operation is either arithmetic or logical, depending on the machine. For unsigned integers, the right shift is logical. (See Appendix H for explanation of these shifts.) The one's complement operator changes each 0 bit to a 1 and each 1 bit to a 0. Parentheses should normally be used with bitwise operators because they are lower in precedence than arithmetic operators. (See the section on precedence later in this chapter.)

		Equivalent in Bits (Binary)	
Expression	*Value*	*Expression*	*Value*
1 | 2	3	00000001 | 00000010	00000011[1]
0xFF&0x0F	0x0F	11111111 & 00001111	00001111[1]
0x33 | 0xCC	0xFF	00110011 | 11001100	11111111[1]
0x0F<<2	0x3C	00001111<<2	00111100[1]
0x1C>>1	0x0E	00011100>>1	00001110[1]
~x03	0xFC	~0000000000000011	1111111111111100[1]

Assignment operator

The use of the assignment operator (=) differentiates C from other languages. Usually the use of the equal sign ("=") in another language with just a variable on one side and an expression on the other defines an assignment statement. That is, "x = y + 3" is a complete statement by itself and cannot be used in other contexts. In C, however, = is an operator that produces a value that can be futher used in an expression. The operator copies the value on the right-hand side into the variable or address on the left-hand side. The result of the operation has a value, which is the value that is transferred and which can be used in other expressions. For example:

Expression	Operation	Value of Expression
i = 3	the value 3 is put in **i**	3
i = 3 + 4	the value 7 is put in **i**	7
i = (k = 4)	the value 4 is put in **k**; the value of the assignment (4) is then put in **i**	4
i = (k = 4) + 3	the value 4 is put in **k**; the addition is performed and the value 7 is put in **i**	7

The assignment operator requires that a variable name or some other expression that points to a memory location be on the left-hand side of the operator. This is called an *lvalue* (for left hand value). For example, if **i** has been declared as **int**, then **i = 5** is valid, and **5 = i** is not valid.

Shorthand assignment

C offers several assignment operators that are shorthand for other operators. These take the form of *op* = where the *op* is + , − ,*,/,%,<<,>>,&,∧, | . The expression *f op* = *g* is the same as *f* = *f op g*.[2] For example:

Expression	Is Equal to
a + =2	a = a+2
j <<=2	j = j<<2
q /=7+2	q = q/(7+2)

Note that the concise form eliminates some of the potential for error in many operations. For example, if one wanted to increment **i** by 2, then:

i = i + 2

would yield the proper result. However it might be possible to mis-key this and enter instead:

i = j + 2

which would yield the value of **j** plus 2. Using:

i + = 2

makes things clearer and is less prone to this type of error. This operator is commonly used with more complicated lvalues, such as elements of arrays or structure members, which are discussed in Chapter 5.

Prefix/postfix operators

There are two operators that are not found in the other languages. These are the postfix and prefix operators. They increment (+ +) or decrement (− −) a single variable. A prefix operation is performed before the value of the variable is used. A postfix operation is performed after the variable is used. For example, for an **int i**:

− −i	pre-decrement **i**
i+ +	post-increment **i**

If **i** had a value of 5, then:

Expression	The Value of i Used in Evaluation	Value of Expression	After Evaluation i Has the Value
5+i+ +	5	10	6
5+i− −	5	10	4
− −i+5	4	9	4
+ +i+5	6	11	6

Conditional operators

Conditional expressions are a shorthand way of selecting one of two values based on the value of another expression. The syntax is:

$$exp1 \ ? \ exp2 : exp3$$

If *exp1* is true (non-zero), then the result is the value of *exp2*. Otherwise it is the value of *exp3*. For example:

Expression	Value
5 ? 1 : 2	1
j ? i+j : k+j	value of **i**+**j** if **j** is non-zero, otherwise the value of **k**+**j**

(m>7) ? 3 : 4	3 if **m** is greater than 7. 4 if **m** is less than or equal to 7
(a>b) ? a : b	the greater of **a** and **b**
(a>b)?((a>c)?a:c):((b>c)?b:c)	the maximum of **a**, **b**, and **c**.

In conditionals, one or the other of the expressions following the **?** is evaluated, but not both.

Comma operator

The comma operator (**,**) does not combine two expressions. It evaluates the two expressions, starting with the left one. The value of a comma-connected expression is the value of the right expression. For example:

Expression	Value
5,6	6
i+ +,j+2	**j**+2

Since it groups from left to right, a string of expressions separated by commas has the value of the right-most expression. The expressions will be evaluated in order from left to right.

Expression	Value
i+ +,j+ +,k+ +	value of **k** (before the increment)
i+ +,j+ +,+ +k	value of **k** (after the increment)

The comma operator is usually used in **while** or **for** statements. (See the section on control-flow in Chapter 3.)

Commas are also used to separate arguments to functions. These commas do not have the same effect as the comma operator and are discussed in Chapter 4.

The operators in other languages corresponding to the C operators are listed in Exhibit 2.3.

TYPE CONVERSIONS

When different types of operands appear in the same expression, automatic conversion to one type is performed. This conversion is determined by a few rules.

In general, character variables and constants are treated as integers in all expressions. For machines on which ASCII is used, their value is the ASCII equivalent of the character. If the character contains a high-order bit of 1, then the resulting integer may have the sign extended or may have the high order bits filled with 0s, depending on the machine. For **unsigned char**, the high-order bits will be filled with zeros. (See Appendix H for a discussion on sign extension and zero filling.)

When evaluating expressions, the following conversions are automatically done:

Type	Converted to	Notes
char and **short**	**int**	sign extension depends on the machine
float	double	all float operations are performed in double precision

Exhibit 2.3 OPERATORS IN OTHER LANGUAGES

C	BASIC	FORTRAN	PASCAL	PL/I	COBOL
+	+	+	+	+	+
−	−	−	−	−	−
*	*	*	*	*	*
/	/	/	/	/	/
− (unary)	−	−	−	−	−
=	=	=	: =	=	=
>	>	.GT.	>	>	>
<	<	.LT.	<	<	<
> =	> =	.GE.	> =	> =	NOT <
< =	< =	.LE.	< =	< =	NOT >
= =	=	.EQ.	=	=	=
! =	<>	.NE.	<>	¬	NOT =
&&	AND	.AND.	AND	&	AND
||	OR	.OR.	OR	|	OR
!	NOT	.NOT.	NOT	¬	NOT
%	MOD	MOD ( )	MOD	MOD( )	
&				&	
|				|	
∧				BOOL ( )	
~				¬	

The following operators have no direct correspondence in the other languages:

<<
>>
+ +
− −
?:
,

When arithmetic operators are evaluated, the operand whose type has the lower position on the following list is converted to the type of the other operand. The value of the result is that of the higher type.

double
long
unsigned
int

If an **int** is converted to a **long**, the sign is extended. If an **unsigned** is converted to a **long**, the high-order bits are zero filled.

For assignment operators, the type of the right-hand expression may need to be converted to the type of the left-hand variable. This is determined by:

Expression Type	Left-Hand Variable	Conversion
double	**float**	rounds off
float	**int**	truncates fractional part; if the number is too big to fit, the result is undetermined

Expression Type	Left-Hand Variable	Conversion
long	int	eliminates high-order bits
int	char	eliminates high-order bits

If a specific type is required, the *cast* construct may be used. Its syntax is:

$$(type)\ exp$$

exp is any expression. The *type* is any data type. Usually this is required in passing values to functions that require particular types. It may also be necessary for some compilers that require more exact typing than does standard C. An example of a cast for **float f = 2.5** is **(int)f**, which has the value of 2.

PRECEDENCE

Operators have an order of precedence. That is, without parenthesis, certain operations are performed before those of lower precedence. For operators with equal precedence, the associativity is left to right, except as shown in the Exhibit 2.4. Grouping with parentheses ensures that the interpretation of the operands proceeds in the order indicated. Each set of operators in Exhibit 2.4 has equal precedence. The symbols not yet covered are described in the following chapters on functions, arrays, and structures.

The precedence rules yield the following interpretations:

Expression	Evaluated as
x + 3*2	x + (3*2)
y = x + 3*2	y = (x + (3*2))
x = y>>5 = = 7	x = ((y>>5) = = 7)
x = y = z	x = (y = z)

The expression **10<<4/2>>1?2:6*2+3&&5||2&1|7** evaluates as **(((10<<(4/2))>>1)?2:((((6*2)+3)&&5)||((2&1)|7))),9** or **2.**

ORDER OF EVALUATION

Note in Exhibit 2.4 that the order of evaluation of the two sides of most operators is not specified. This means that if **int x = 5;** then **(++x) + (--x)** has the values $5+4 = 9$ if right side is evaluated first, or $6+5 = 11$ if left side is evaluated first. Depending on the compiler, either value is possible.

STATEMENTS

An executable statement in C is any valid expression followed by a semicolon (**;**). Thus:

Expression	Statement	Notes
a = 5	a = 5;	Puts 5 into variable **a**
7	7;	Does nothing
j = i + 3	j = i + 3;	Adds 3 to value of **i** and puts the result in **j**

Exhibit 2.4 PRECEDENCE OF OPERATORS

Operator		Associativity	Order of Evaluation
( )	function call	left to right	
[ ]	array element		
->	pointer to structure member		
.	structure member		
!	logical negation	right to left	
~	one's complement		
++	increment		
--	decrement		
-	unary minus		
(type**)**	cast		
*	pointer		
&	address		
sizeof	size of object		
*	multiplication	left to right	
/	division		
%	modulus		
+	addition	left to right	
-	subtraction		
<<	left shift	left to right	
>>	right shift		
<	less than	left to right	
<=	less than or equal to		
>	greater than		
>=	greater than or equal to		
==	equality	left to right	
!=	inequality		
&	bitwise AND	left to right	
∧	bitwise XOR	left to right	
|	bitwise OR	left to right	
&&	logical AND	left to right	left to right
||	logical OR	left to right	left to right
?:	conditional	right to left	
=	assignment	right to left	
op =	assignment		
,	comma	left to right	left to right

Exhibit 2.5 COMPOUND STATEMENTS IN OTHER LANGUAGES

BASIC

Statements on a single line that are separated by colons (:) and statements in FOR loops have some of the properties of a compound statement.

FORTRAN

The statements in DO loops have some of the properties of a compound statement.

PASCAL

```
BEGIN
    . . .
END;
```

PL/I

```
BEGIN;         DO;
  . . . and       . . .
END;           END;
```

COBOL

PERFORMing a paragraph is similar to executing a compound statement.

A statement may consist of just a semicolon (;). This is the null statement, which is used for special purposes, such as a place to branch for a **goto**. (See Chapter 3.)

Compound statements

A compound statement is one or more simple statements surrounded by braces ({ and }). The compound statement, also called a block, can appear anywhere a single statement can be used. It is usually used for bodies of loops, such as the **while** loop. The syntax is:

```
{
zero or more statements
}
```

An example of compound statement is:

```
{
i=j;
j++;
}
```

Exhibit 2.5 shows the equivalent of compound statements in other languages.

WHITE SPACE

Unlike some other languages, C is free-form in its writing. Spaces, ends of lines, and tabs (i.e., *white space*) are ignored for the most part. Only in special instances, such as keywords and character strings, is white space significant. For example:

Statement	Interpretation
int i;	declares **i** to be an integer
inti;	the value of the variable **inti** or declaration of the variable **inti**

What white space is shown in programs is mostly for human readability. For example, statements do not have to be on separate lines. The compound statement { **i=j; j+ +; }** is valid. Suggested rules for placement of tabs and braces are discussed in Chapter 9.

Comments

Non-executable comments are surrounded by /* and */. Any characters may be within a comment. The compiler treats comments as white space and ignores them. Most compilers do not permit comments to be nested. Examples of comments are:

/* **This is a comment** */

/*

    This
    is
    also
    a
    comment

Footnotes

1. The high order bits of these equivalents are all 0. 2. An obsolete syntax for the *op=* operator is *=op*. This may appear in older C programs, but should not be used in new ones. 3. COBOL numbers are kept in BCD (Binary Coded Decimal) format (except for computationals). BCD numbers do not have direct equivalents in C. A close approximation has been made.

3
Control Flow

As with many other languages, the flow of control in a C program is sequential. Statements are executed from first to last, unless a specific control statement changes the order. All programs begin with the first statement of the function "main ( )." Three control structures are commonly used in writing structured programs. These are the *if-then-else* form (i.e., if a condition is true, do this, else do that), the *while* form (i.e., execute a sequence of instructions repeatedly while some condition is met), and the *case* form (i.e., execute only one of several sets of instructions based on some value). Some languages provide one or two of these. C has them all, as well as a couple of others and the universal *goto*.

IF

The first construct is the **if** statement. The **if** tests for the logical true or false value of a given expression. If the expression is true, the statement following the **if** is executed. Otherwise control is transferred to the instruction following the statement. The construct is shown in Flowchart 3.1. The syntax is:

    if (*exp*) *stmt*

The expression *exp* is evaluated. If it is non-zero (true), then statement *stmt* is executed.

Example	Action
if (x = = 5) y = 3;	If **x** has the value of 5 (making the expression **x = = 5** have a value of 1, or true), then the value of 3 is placed in **y**

Exhibit 3.1 gives the equivalent of the **if** statement in other languages.

The **if-else** allows one of two alternatives to be executed based on the value of an expression. Flowchart 3.2 diagrams this. The syntax for this is:

    if (*exp*)
        stmt1
    else
        stmt2

Flowchart 3.1 IF

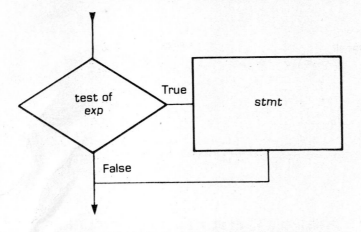

Exhibit 3.1 IF IN OTHER LANGUAGES

BASIC

10 IF (X = 5) THEN Y = 3

FORTRAN

IF (X.EQ.5) Y = 3

PASCAL

IF (X = 5) THEN Y: = 3;

PL/I

IF (X = 5) THEN Y = 3;

COBOL

IF X EQUALS 5 THEN COMPUTE Y = 3.

For example, suppose that if **x** is less than 6, **y** is to be set to 1 else **y** is to be set to 2.

```
if (x<6)
        y=1;
else
        y=2;
```

This corresponds to the constructs in other languages in Exhibit 3.2.

if statements may be nested (i.e., an **if** statement can have an **if** itself). Without clarifying brackets, the compiler assumes that an **else** statement belongs to the last **if** used. For example:

Flowchart 3.2 IF-ELSE

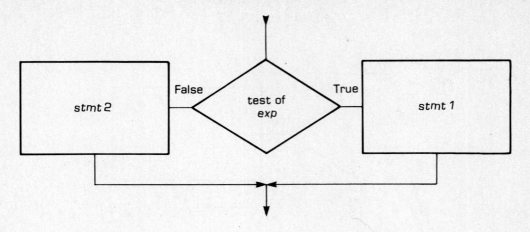

Exhibit 3.2 IF-ELSE IN OTHER LANGUAGES

BASIC

```
10 Y = 1
20 IF (X > = 6) THEN Y = 2
```

or

```
10 IF (X < 6) THEN Y = 1
20 IF (X > = 6) THEN Y = 2[1]
```

or

```
10 IF (X < 6) THEN Y = 1 : GOTO 30
20 Y = 2
30 . . .
```

MBASIC

```
10 IF (X < 6) THEN Y = 1 ELSE Y = 2
```

FORTRAN

```
Y = 1
IF (X.GE.6) Y = 2
```

PASCAL

```
IF X < 6 THEN
    Y : = 1
ELSE
    Y : = 2;
```

PL/I

```
IF X < 6 THEN
    Y = 1;
ELSE
    Y = 2;
```

Exhibit 3.2 continued

COBOL

```
IF X LESS THAN 6 THEN
        COMPUTE Y = 1
ELSE
        COMPUTE Y = 2
```

```
if (i>2)
     if (j= =3)
          y=4;
     else y=  5;
```

means that if **i** is greater than 2 and **j** is not equal to 3, then the value 5 will be put in **y**. Flowchart 3.3 gives the flow of this code.

```
if (i>2)
     {
     if (j= =3)
          y=4;
     }
     else y=5;
```

means if **i** is less than or equal to 2, 5 will be placed in **y**. Flowchart 3.4 gives the flow of this code.

Flowchart 3.3 EXAMPLE OF IF-ELSE

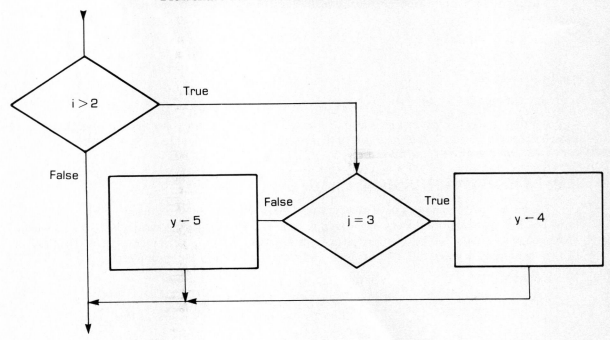

Flowchart 3.4 EXAMPLE OF IF-ELSE

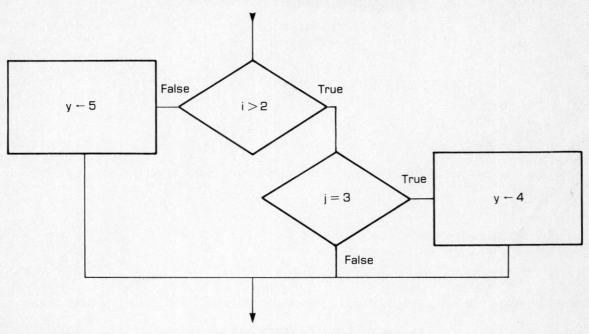

The conditional expression introduced in the last chapter can be used instead of some simple **if** statements. For example:

```
if (a>b) c=a;
else c=b;
```

can be replaced by:

```
c=(a>b ? a : b);
```

A string of **if-else**s that test the value of a integer variable against constants can be replaced by the **switch** construct, which is described later in this chapter.

THE TEST EXPRESSION

The test of the expression in the **if** construct (and the other structured constructs) uses the value of 0 for false and non-zero for true. Many languages require a relational expression of the form "something compared to something" as "if a>b" (if a is greater than b) or "if a=b" (if a is equal to b). The flexibility of C in permitting any expression to be used can be error provoking. For example:

Example	Action
if (i==3) y=5;	If the value of **i** is 3, then 5 is put in **y**.
if (i=3) y=5;	The value 3 is put in **i**. The result (3) is a "true" value so 5 is put into **y**.

Since the test is of any expression, there is a shorthand for testing for a non-zero value.

if (i! = 0) y = 3;

is equivalent to

if (i) y = 3;

WHILE

The next conditional construct is the **while**. The **while** allows the repetition of a statement or block of code until some condition is false. Something inside the body of the **while** must cause the condition to go false or the loop will continue endlessly.[2] The **break** statement described later can be used to exit an endless **while** loop. The flow of a **while** is shown in Flowchart 3.5. The **while** syntax is:

while (exp)
stmt

The statement *stmt* is called the body of the loop. The body may not even be executed once if the expression *exp* is false (a zero value) the first time. A **while** example is:

```
i = 0;
while (i<5)
        i + +;
```

Flowchart 3.5 WHILE

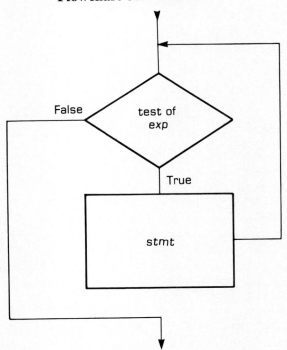

i is set to 0. The expression **i<5** evaluates to a true value (1) and the body of the **while** (the **i+ +;**) is executed. The body will be executed five times, then the next statement in the program executed. On exit, **i** will have the value of 5.

```
i=5;
while (i)
     i− −;
```

i is set to 5. The expression **i** first evaluates to a 5 (true) so the body (the **i− −;**) is executed. This loop will also be executed five times. On exit, **i** will have the value of 0.

```
j=0;
i=0;
while (i<5)
     {
     j = j +2;
     i+ +;
     }
```

This is an example of a compound statement following the **while**. Both statements will be executed until the expression **i<5** turns false (i.e., when **i** gets incremented to 5);

The **while** loop is found in most of the other languages. Equivalent code for the above example is given in Exhibit 3.3.

Exhibit 3.3 WHILE IN OTHER LANGUAGES

BASIC

```
10 J=0
20 I=0
30 IF (I>=5) GOTO 70
40 J=J+2
50 I=I+1
60 GOTO 30
70 . . .
```

MBASIC

```
10 J=0
20 I=0
30 WHILE (I<5)
40 J=J+2
50 I=I+2
60 WEND
```

FORTRAN

```
   J=0
   I=0
30 IF (I.GE.5) GOTO 70
   J=J+2
   I=I+1
   GOTO 30
70 . . .
```

Exhibit 3.3 continued

PASCAL

```
J := 0;
I := 0;
WHILE (I<5) DO
      BEGIN
            J := J+2;
            I := I+1
      END;
```

PL/I

```
J=0;
I=0;
DO WHILE (I<5) ;
      J=J+2;
      I=I+1;
      END;
```

COBOL

```
COMPUTE J=0.
COMPUTE I=0.
PERFORM INC
      UNTIL I IS GREATER THAN 5 OR I IS EQUAL TO 5
      . . .
INC.
      COMPUTE J=J+2.
      COMPUTE I=I+1.
```

DO-WHILE

If it is required that a **while** loop be run through at least once, then values could be set such that the test expression initially is a non-zero value. For example, for the following **while** loop, the value of **i** must be initially set to greater than 5 if the body of the **while** is to be executed one time.

```
j=4;
i=6;
while (i>5)
      {
      i=j--;
      }
```

The **do-while** construct avoids this problem. It operates much like the **while**, but the body of the loop will be always executed one or more times. The syntax is:

```
do
      stmt
while (exp);
```

Flowchart 3.6 DO-WHILE

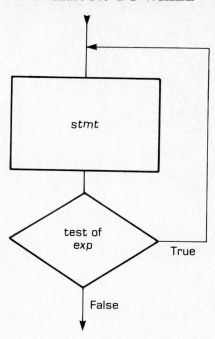

Note that the semicolon (;) following the expression *exp* after the **while** is required. Flowchart 3.6 illustrates the **do-while**. Using this construct, the example above can be written as:

```
j=4;
do
    i=j--;
    while (i>5);
```

The loop will be executed once. The expression **i>5** will be found false. **j** will have a value of 3 upon exiting the loop.

The equilvalent of the **do-while** in other languages is shown in Exhibit 3.4

FOR

Although the **while** is sufficient for a structured program, a similar construct appears frequently enough to have a separate structure. The sequence of operations is as follows: set some initial variable; perform the body of a loop; increment the variable; if the new value is less than a terminating value, perform the loop again. This sequence is embodied in Flowchart 3.7. In C, this construct is the **for**. Its syntax is:

```
for (exp1;exp2;exp3)
    stmt
```

Exhibit 3.4 DO-WHILE IN OTHER LANGUAGES

BASIC

```
10 J=4
20 I=J
30 J=J−1
40 IF (I>5) GOTO 20
```

FORTRAN

```
   J=4
10 I=J
   J=J−1
   IF (I>5) GOTO 10
```

PASCAL

```
J=4;
REPEAT
    I=J;
    J=J−1
UNTIL I<=5;
```

PL/I

```
J=4;
DO UNTIL (I<=5);
    I=J;
    J=J−1;
    END;
```

COBOL

```
    COMPUTE J=4.
    COMPUTE I=6.
    PERFORM INC. UNTIL I<=5.
        . . .
INC.
    COMPUTE I=J.
    COMPUTE J=J−1.
```

For example, the following loop will be executed five times:

```
for (i=0;i<5;i++)
    j++;
```

The equivalent loop in other languages is shown in Exhibit 3.5. In some languages, the loop control variable (such as **i** above) is a temporary variable that cannot be altered inside the loop. Its value may be undefined upon exiting the loop. C has neither of these properties. In a few languages, the control variable must be an integer. It may be any type in C.

The **for** can decrement the variable as well as increment it. For example:

```
for (i=5;i>0;i−−)
    j=j*2;
```

Flowchart 3.7 FOR

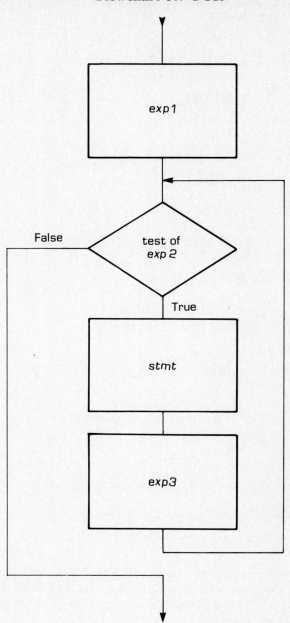

Exhibit 3.5 FOR IN OTHER LANGUAGES

BASIC

```
10 FOR I = 1 TO 5 STEP 1
20 J = J + 1
30 NEXT I
```

FORTRAN

```
     DO 10 I = 1,5,1
     J = J + 1
10 CONTINUE
```

PASCAL

```
     FOR I : = 1 TO 5 DO
          J : = J + 1;
```

PL/I

```
     DO I = 1 TO 5 BY 1;
          J = J + 1;
          END;
```

COBOL

```
     PERFORM INC VARYING I FROM 1 TO 5 BY 1.
               . . .
INC.
     COMPUTE J = J + 1.
```

The two semicolons in the **for** are required. However, any or all of the expressions may be omitted.

```
        for (;;)
            ;
```

is equivalent to

```
        while (1)
            ;
```

and

```
        for (;i<5;)
            i + +;
```

is the same as

```
        while (i<5)
            i + +;
```

Since expressions can be connected by comma operators, it is possible to put much of the loop in the **for** statement itself. For example:

```
        for (i = 0;i<5;i + +)
            j + +;
```

could be written as

```
for (i=0;i<5;j+ +,i+ +)
    ;
```

The final semicolon (;) is a null statement, which is the body of the loop. Note that the comma operator in a **for** is normally used for double indexing of arrays and similar operations.

CONTINUE

With **for**, **while**, and **do-while**, it is often convenient to be able to skip to the end of the loop and perform the test again without executing intermediate instructions. The **continue** instruction permits one to do this. With the **for** loop, the **continue** passes control to the increment or decrement expression, rather than going directly to the test. Flowchart 3.8 shows an example of a **continue** in the body of a **for**. The code for the example is:

```
j=0;
for (i=0;i<5;i+ +)
    {
    if (i>3) continue;
    j+ +;
    }
```

When the value of **i** exceeds 3, the **j+ +** statement will be skipped. The loop will be executed 5 times. However the incrementing of **j** will only be done four times. Upon exiting the loop, **j** will have the value 4, and **i** will have the value of 5.

BREAK

Sometimes it is necessary to break out of a loop without performing the termination test. The **break** instruction permits this. An example of a **break** in a loop is shown in Flowchart 3.9. The code for this example is:

```
j=0;
for (i=0;i<5;i+ +)
    {
    if (j>2) break;
    j+ +;
    }
```

When the value of **j** exceeds 2, control will be passed to the next statement outside the **for** loop. The **if** (**j>2**) test will be executed 4 times. On exiting, **j** will have the value of 3, and **i** will have the value of 3.

In nested loops, **break** only exits out of the innermost loop. To break out of several nested loops, a **goto** is more practical.

Flowchart 3.8 EXAMPLE OF CONTINUE

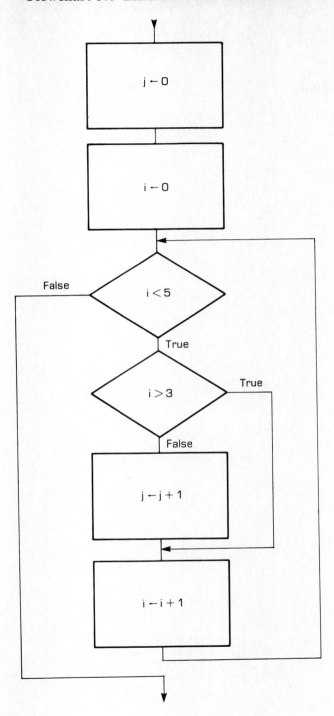

Flowchart 3.9 EXAMPLE OF BREAK

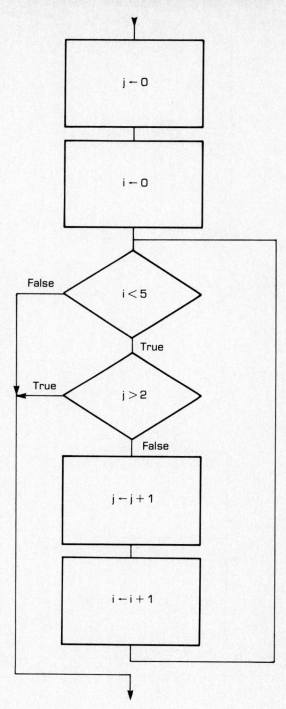

Flowchart 3.10 SWITCH (NO BREAKS)

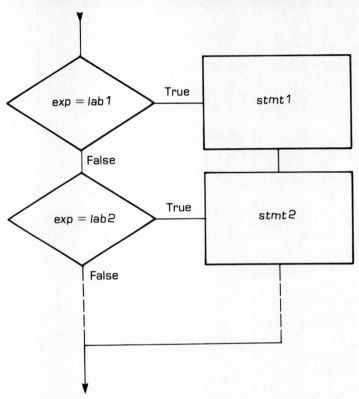

SWITCH

If the value of an integer expression is being tested multiple times, as with nested **if** statements, the **switch** construct will make the code both clearer and faster. The **switch** operates as shown in Flowchart 3.10. It computes the value of an expression and branches to the **case** label equal to that value. Its syntax is:

```
switch (integer expression)
    {
case lab1:
        stmt1 (optional)
case lab2:
        stmt2 (optional)
    . . .
    }
```

Each label must be an integer constant or an expression composed only of integer constants that can be evaluated by the compiler. If no label matches the value of the expression, then no statements are executed in the switch. A label of **default** can be used to identify statements to be executed in case none of the other cases match. For example:

```
switch (i)
    {
    case 1:
        j=j+5;
    case 2:
    case 3:
        j=j+3;
    }
```

If Value of i Is:	Statements Executed
1	j=j+5; j=j+3;
2 or 3	j=j+3;
anything else	none

The **break** instruction is commonly used to end the statements following each **case** label. Use of it makes the **switch** correspond to the structured "case" statement. For example:

```
switch(i)
    {
    case 1:
        j=j+5;
        break;
    case 2:
    case 3:
        j=j+3;
        break;
    default:
        j=j+1;
    }
```

If Value of i Is:	Statements Executed
1	j=j+5;
2 or 3	j=j+3;
anything else	j=j+1;

See Exhibit 3.6 for the equivalent of this **switch** example in other languages. Flowchart 3.11 illustrates the flow of this code.

The nested **if** statement that this **switch** is equivalent to is:

```
if (i==1) j=j+5;
else if ((i==2) || (i==3)) j=j+3;
else j=j+1;
```

The **switch** code appears somewhat clearer than this form. In addition, the **switch** will usually execute faster.

Exhibit 3.6 SWITCH WITH BREAKS IN OTHER LANGUAGES

BASIC

```
5   ON (I) GOTO 10,20,20
7   GOTO 30
10 J=J+5
15 GOTO 40
20 J=J+3
25 GOTO 40
30 J=J+1
40 CONTINUE
```

FORTRAN

```
      GO TO (10,20,20), I
      GOTO 30
10 J=J+5
      GO TO 40
20 J=J+3
      GO TO 40
30 J=J+1
40 CONTINUE
```

PASCAL

```
CASE I OF
      1:   J := J+5;
      2,3: J := J+3;
      END
```

There is no default case for standard PASCAL.

PL/I

```
SELECT (I);
      WHEN (1) J = J+5;
      WHEN (2,3) J = J+3;
      OTHERWISE J= J+1;
      END;
```

COBOL

```
      GO TO A
            B
            B
            DEPENDING ON I.
      COMPUTE J = J+1.
      GO TO C.
A. COMPUTE J=J+5.
      GO TO C.
B. COMPUTE J=J+3.
      GO TO C.
C. . . .
```

Flowchart 3.11 SWITCH (WITH BREAKS)

GOTO

Devotees of structured programming reel with horror when someone mentions the GOTO. This statement is designed to alter the sequential flow of the program. Although it can be improperly used so as to make code completely unreadable (commonly termed "spaghetti code"), it sometimes appears even in the best of highly structured code for particular purposes.

The **goto** works just like the *goto* in other languages. It transfers the execution of a program to another statement in the program. The statement to which control is transferred must be identified by a label. The syntax is:

Exhibit 3.7 GOTO IN OTHER LANGUAGES

BASIC

```
10  GOTO 50
    . . .
50 Y = 3
```

FORTRAN

```
   GOTO 50
    . . .
50 Y = 3
```

PASCAL

```
    GOTO 50
    . . .
50: Y = 3;
```

PL/I

```
    GOTO LAB;
     . . .
LAB: Y = 3;
```

COBOL

```
    GOTO LAB.
     . . .
LAB.
    COMPUTE Y = 3.
```

goto *lab*;   for the goto
lab: *stmt*   for the label

For example:

    goto LAB;   control transfers to statement labeled **LAB**
    . . .
    LAB: y = 3;

In other languages, the same thing is possible as shown in Exhibit 3.7.

Footnotes

1. Note in BASIC, that if the block of code following the IF affects the value being tested, then the second form of the BASIC example must be avoided. Cases like this can be a trap. For example, if X is less than 6 it is to be set to 7, else it should be set to 5. 2. In computers that execute more than one program simultaneously, a second program might perform an operation that would set the expression of the **while** loop false.

    10 IF (X<6) X = 7
    20 IF (X> = 6) X = 5

Functions

Functions in C are used for the same purpose as functions and subroutines in other languages. The C function combines the features of both. The C function is a subroutine that returns a value that may be used in an expression.[1] Unlike some other languages, function definitions in C may not be nested within other functions. All program blocks in C are functions.

FUNCTION DEFINITION

The syntax for defining a function is

> *type name(formal parameters)*
> *declarations of formal parameters*
> {
> *declarations of variables*
> *statements*
> }

The *type* determines the type of return value. This will be described later in this chapter. The names of the formal parameters are separated by commas. If the declaration of a formal parameter is omitted, the parameter is assumed to be of type **int**. The names of the formal parameters can be used within the function just as any variable of their type. The initial values of the parameters are set when the function is called.

The **return** statement in a function ends the execution of the function and returns a value to the calling expression. If the end of the function (the closing brace }) is reached without a **return** statement being executed, there is an assumed return. The **return** syntax is:

> **return** *exp*;

If the expression *exp* is missing or if there is no **return**, the value returned is undefined. An example function is:

```
addone(innum)
int innum;
    {
```

Exhibit 4.1 FUNCTIONS IN OTHER LANGUAGES

BASIC

```
5   DEF FN AD(IN) = IN + 1                          function definition
10 AN = FN AD(5)                                    function call
```

FORTRAN

```
INTEGER FUNCTION ADDONE(INNUM)                      function definition
INTEGER INNUM
ADDONE = INNUM + 1
RETURN
END

ANSWER = ADDONE(5)                                  function call
```

PASCAL

```
FUNCTION ADDONE(INNUM : INTEGER) : INTEGER:         function definition
BEGIN
        ADDONE : = INNUM + 1
END;

ANSWER : = ADDONE(5);                               function call
```

PL/I

```
ADDONE: PROCEDURE(INNUM) RETURNS                    function definition
   (FIXED(15,0));
DECLARE INNUM FIXED(15,0);
DECLARE OUTNUM FIXED(15,0);
BEGIN;
        OUTNUM = INNUM + 1;
        RETURN (OUTNUM);
END ADDONE;

ANSWER = ADDONE(5);                                 function call
```

COBOL

Nothing equivalent

```
int outnum;
outnum = innum +1;
return outnum;
}
```

addone receives a value in **innum**, puts that value plus one into **outnum**, and returns the value of **outnum**.

To call a function, the syntax is:

name(actual parameters)

If the above function was defined, then in another part of the program, one could use:

Expression	Value
addone(5)	6
5+addone(4)	10

A valid statement would be:

answer = addone(5);

The corresponding elements in other languages are shown in Exhibit 4.1.

ARGUMENTS

C normally uses a "call by value" system of argument passing. This means that copies of the values of the arguments in the calling expression are supplied to the function. The function cannot change the value of the arguments in the calling routine. The values passed to a function undergo the same conversions as in expressions. That is, all **char** and **short** values are converted to **int** values and all **float** values are converted to **double** before they are passed.

A routine may use the formal arguments as temporary local variables. For example, if

```
addone(innum)
int innum;
    {
    innum + = 1;
    return innum;
    }
```

is called by

```
int i = 5;
int j;
. . .
j = addone(i);
```

the value of **i** in the calling routine does not change.

Call by reference

C also allows "call by reference." The called function can be supplied the memory address (a reference) of the argument, rather than the value of the argument. The function can then change the value of the variable in the calling routine by using this address. Both the function and the calling program must be informed that an argument is called by reference by using the operators **&** (for passing the address) and **∗** (for receiving an address). The **&** and ∗ symbols will be explained more in Chapter 6. For example, if a function was defined:

```
increase(innum)
int *innum;
    {
    (*innum) + + ;
    return;
    }
```

it might be called from another program by a statement such as:

int out=5;

. . .

increase(&out);

After the function was executed, the value of **out** would be 6.

Subroutines in other languages usually use the call by reference method of argument passing. The routines in other languages that are equivalent to this example are shown in Exhibit 4.2.

A function does not have to have any arguments. A perfectly valid function definition is:

nothing( )

{

return 0;

}

so then in calling routine **nothing** ( ) has the value of 0.

Branching to and returning from C functions without any parameter passing is usually as quick as the assembly language ''branch to subroutine'' and ''return from subroutine'' instructions for a given computer.

RETURN VALUES

By default, a function is assumed to return an integer value. If a function returns other than that type of value, it must be declared as such in both the definition and in the calling routine. To define the type of value returned by a function, the name of the function is preceded by the type. The value of the expression following **return** is converted to that type. For example:

double faddone(fin)

double fin;

{

double fout;

fout=fin+1.;

return fout;

}

defines a function that returns a **double** value. In the calling routine, the function must be declared to return a value of that type. If the above function were used, the calling routine should include in its declarations the statement:

double faddone( );

Then **faddone** can be called by:

Expression	Value
faddone(5.)	6.
faddone((double)5)	6.

Note that the actual parameters in the calling program should agree in number and type with the formal parameters. With the above function, a call to **faddone(5)** (i.e., an integer 5) would result in **faddone**

Exhibit 4.2 SUBROUTINES IN OTHER LANGUAGES

BASIC

```
5   OU=5
10 GOSUB 50                                    subroutine call
        . . .
50 OU=OU+1                                     subroutine definition
60 RETURN
```

FORTRAN

```
SUBROUTINE INCREASE(INNUM)                     subroutine
INTEGER INNUM
INNUM=INNUM+1
RETURN
END

CALL INCREASE (OUT)                            subroutine call
```

PASCAL

```
PROCEDURE INCREASE(VAR INNUM:INTEGER);         subroutine
BEGIN
        INNUM := INNUM+1
END;

INCREASE(OUT);                                 subroutine call
```

PL/I

```
INCREASE: PROCEDURE (INNUM);                   subroutine
DECLARE INNUM FIXED(15,0);
INNUM=INNUM+1;
RETURN;
END INCREASE;

CALL INCREASE(OUT);                            subroutine call
```

COBOL

```
IDENTIFICATION DIVISION.                       subroutine
PROG-ID.
        INCREASE.
        . . .
ENVIRONMENT DIVISION.
DATA DIVISION.
LINKAGE SECTION.
        . . .
01 INNUM PICTURE 99999.
        . . .
PROCEDURE DIVISION USING INNUM.
        COMPUTE INNUM=INNUM+1.
        EXIT PROGRAM.
        . . . .

        CALL'INCREASE' USING OUT.              subroutine call
```

receiving a garbage value due to the type mismatch and therefore it would return garbage value. Similarly a call of **faddone( )** would also result in garbage being received and returned. Since actual arguments of types **char** are converted to **int** and **float** are converted to **double**, formal parameters are usually never declared as **char** and **float**.

C interprets the use of a name followed by ( ) with or without arguments as an implicit declaration of a function that returns an integer. Thus functions that return integer values do not need to be declared in the calling routine.

The UNIX C compiler allows the declaration of a function that returns a type of **void**. This is used for functions that do not return values. The compiler uses this information to ensure that values returned from such functions are not used in expressions.

EXAMPLE FUNCTIONS

These are some example functions. There are many more in the next two chapters.

chklim

This routine checks to see if a value is between two limits.

```
chklim(num,low,high)
/*  returns 1 if num between low and high
    else returns 0 */
int num; /* number to check */
int low; /* low limit */
int high; /* high limit */
    {
    int ret=0;
    if (num>=low)
        {
        if (num<=high) ret=1;
        else ret=0;
        }
    else  ret=0;
    return ret;
    }
```

This could be also written as:

```
chklim(num,low,high)
        /*  returns 1 if num is between low and high
            else returns 0 */
        int num; /* number to check */
        int low; /* low limit */
        int high; /* high limit */
            {
            return ( (num>=low) && (num<=high));
            }
```

power

This routine raises a floating number to an integer power.

```
double power (d,n)
/* raises number to an integer power */
double d; /* number to raise to power */
int n;      /* power to raise it to */
    {
    double ret;
    ret=1.;
    /* if power is negative, use 1/d */
    if (n<0)
        {
        n= -n;
        d=1./d;
        }
    while (n- -)
        {
        ret *= d;
        }
    return ret;
    }
```

Sample functions from the C library

Several character-oriented functions are usually included in C compiler libraries. Possible source code for these functions follows. Note that these functions work for the ASCII character set. Other character representations may not work.

isdigit(chr) returns a value not equal to 0 if **chr** is a digit. Otherwise it returns a value of 0. It might be implemented as:

```
isdigit(chr)
/* returns 0 if chr is not a digit
     non-zero if chr is a digit */
int chr; /* character to test */
    {
    int ret;
    if ((chr>='0')&&(chr<='9')) ret=1;
    else  ret=0;
    return ret;
    }
```

or

```
isdigit(chr)
int chr;
    {
    return ((chr>='0')&&(chr<='9'));
    }
```

toupper(chr) returns the upper case value of **chr** if **chr** is a lower case character. Otherwise it returns the value of **chr**. Possible code for it is:

```
toupper(chr)
/* returns upper case character if chr is lower case, else returns chr */
int chr; /* character to test */
    {
    int sub;
    if ((chr>='a')&&(chr<='z')) sub='a'-'A';
    else sub=0;
    return chr-sub;
    }
```

or

```
toupper(chr)
int chr;
    {
    return ( (chr>='a') && (chr<='z') ?
        chr-('a'-'A') : chr);
    }
```

PROGRAMS

A program in C is a collection of one or more functions. One and only one function must be named **main**. This is the first function that will be called when the program is executed. Functions can communicate values to one another by parameter lists, return values, and external variables (to be described next).

Unlike Pascal and a few other languages, functions cannot be nested within functions. Each function stands alone.

A short program that uses the example function **power** described previously is:

```
main( )
/* raises a number to a power */
    {
    double power ( );
    float fin;
    int iin;
    float result;
    printf("\nInput the float ");
    scanf("%f",&fin);
    printf("\nInput the power ");
    scanf("%d",&iin);
    result=power(fin,iin);
    printf("\nResult is %f ",result);
    exit(0);
    }

double power (d,n)
/* raises number to an integer power */
double d; /* number to raise to power */
int n;      /* power to raise it to */
    {
```

```
double ret;
ret = 1.;
/* if power is negative, use 1/d */
if (n<0)
    {
    n = -n;
    d = 1./d;
    }
while (n - -)
    {
    ret *= d;
    }
return ret;
}
```

EXTERNALS

Functions are not limited to passing values through their parameter lists. Like most other languages, C supports external or global variables. Any variable declaration that appears outside of a function is taken to be the definition of an external variable. For example:

```
int outside;
funct( )
    {
    . . .
    }
```

defines **outside** to be an external variable of type **int** and assigns storage to it. **outside** can be referenced by any function in this source file that comes after its definition. The variable may be initialized to a value in this definition, as

```
int outside = 5;
funct( )
    {
    . . .
    }
```

If it is not explicitly initialized, an external variable will have an initial value of $0.$[2]

Like most other languages, C source files can be compiled separately into relocatable object files and then linked together later into a executable file. (See Appendix J for a discussion of compilation and linking.) An external variable should be defined in only one source file. In any other source files, reference can be made to it by declaring it as an **extern** variable. The **extern** declaration does not assign storage to the variable. It informs the compiler that the variable will be defined elsewhere as an external. For example, :

```
extern int outside;
func1( )
    {
    . . .
    }
```

declares **outside** to be an external variable of type **int**. This variable must be defined in a source file that will be linked into the final program or an "undefined external" message will be given by the linker.

If an external variable definition appears in a source file after the definition of a function that references it, then that function must include an **extern** declaration for the variable. The convention of putting all external definitions at the beginning of a source file avoids this difficulty.[3]

The equivalent of externals in other languages is shown in Exhibit 4.3.

The fact that source files that make up a program can be separately compiled allows an additional type of external variable called the **static** external. It is an external variable known only within the source file in which it is declared. As with externals, **static** externals are only known from the point of the definition onwards. Since **static** externals are usually declared at the top of the program, this is equivalent to being known throughout the file. For example:

```
static int secret;
funct1( )
    {
    secret + + ;
    . . .
    }
```

declares **secret** to be a **static** external **int** variable. The variable will not be known outside this source file. Even if another function had an **extern** declaration of **secret**, that variable would not be linked to this one. This permits "information hiding."

Exhibit 4.3 EXTERNALS IN OTHER LANGUAGES

BASIC

All variables in a program are global.

MBASIC

Common variables in chained programs are global among programs

FORTRAN

COMMON OUTSIDE

PASCAL

All identifiers declared in the main program are global.
All identifiers declared within a procedure are hidden from external procedures, but are globally known by procedures nested within it.

PL/I

DECLARE OUTSIDE EXTERNAL FIXED BIN(15,0);
All identifiers declared within a procedure are hidden from external procedures, but are globally known by procedures nested within it.

COBOL

LINKAGE SECTION.
    . . .
    01 OUTSIDE PICTURE 99999.

A common coding practice is to put **extern** declarations of all external variables in a single source file and then to include this file in the other files using the **#include** compiler instruction described in Chapter 7.

Example program

This program computes an average of the input numbers. The two routines **iniavg** and **avg** use the external variables **sum** and **count** to communicate with each other. Although **count** and **sum** are implicitly initialized to **0**, the **iniavg** routine has been supplied in case more than one set of averages was wanted.

```
main ( )
/* this program computes the running average of input numbers */
/* an input of 0 or a bad input terminates the program */
    {
    float f,avg;
    double averag( );
    int ret;
    printf("\nThis program computes running averages");
    iniavg( );

    do
        {
        printf("\nEnter a number. Enter 0 to end: ");
        ret = scanf("%f",&f);
        if ((f! = 0.0)&&(ret = = 1))
            {
            avg = averag(f);
            printf("\nAverage so far is %f",avg);
            }
        }
        while ((f! = 0.0)&&(ret = = 1));
    exit(0);
    }
int count;
double sum;
iniavg( )
/* initializes the averaging for averag( ) */
    {
    sum = 0.0;
    count = 0;
    return;
    }
double averag(f)
/* averages the input numbers returns average */
double f; /* number to be averaged in */
    {
    sum + = f;
    count + + ;
    return sum/count;
    }
```

Now, if desired, these two routines could be kept in another source file and put into a library, so they could be used by other programs. If that were the case, then the declarations for **count** and **sum** should read:

```
static int count;
static float sum;
```

Then the names **count** and **sum** would never get confused with variables of the same names used as externals in other source files.

SCOPE OF NAMES

Variable declarations can be made any time an opening brace ({) appears, as in a function or compound statement. Any declarations made are good until the closing brace (}). Diagram 4.1 gives a layout of the scope of names. An example is:

```
float k = 0.0;
func1( )
    {
    . . .
    k = 1.;                refers to the external k
    . . .
    }
func2( )
    {
    char k;
    . . .
    k = 'b';               refers to char k
    while (1)
        {
        int k = 2;
        k + +;             refers to int k
        . . .
        }
    k = 'a';               refers to char k
    . . .
    }
```

Each time a new declaration for **k** appears, it defines a new **auto** variable. Each nested block refers only to the declaration of **k** within it.

Labels names have the same scope as variable names. A label can be redefined in any nested compound statement in a routine. Ease of code maintenance suggests not using this feature.

Function names are globally known through all files that are linked together. A function can be declared **static** to make it known only within a source file. Then a call to that function from another source file will not be linked to that function definition.[5]

Diagram 4.1 SCOPE OF NAMES

OUTSIDE A FUNCTION

type x;	this may be referenced within this source file and by other source files using the **extern** declaration[4]
static *type x*	this may be referenced only with this source file[4]
extern *type x*	this must be defined in another source file[4]

INSIDE A FUNCTION

these may be referenced only within this function and nested blocks

```
func ()
    {
    static type x
    auto type x
    type x            (defaults to auto)
    register type x
    extern type x
    }
```

INSIDE A COMPOUND STATEMENT

these may be referenced only within this block and nested blocks

```
    {
    static type x
    auto type x
    type x            (defaults to auto)
    register type x
    extern type x
    }
```

Footnotes

1. In general, a function is a subprogram that returns a value. It can be called within an expression. A subroutine is a subprogram that does not return a value. It is called in some languages by the CALL statement. Another difference is that a function does not usually change the values of the arguments with which it is called and a subroutine does change the value of at least one argument.

The ability to enter a subprogram not only at the top, but also at any place in it is included in some languages. C does not have this feature, but the keyword **entry** is a reserved word. It is not implemented in any compiler and will probably not be used in the future. 2. In order to save space in the executable file, some compilers do not initialize large external arrays to 0. 3. Some compilers eliminate the distinction between **extern** declarations and multiple definitions of external variables in source files. The multiple definitions do not produce errors, but simply reference to the same variable. 4. This can be only referenced within the source file by routines that come after its appearance. Some compilers are not this particular. 5. Technically, this function name will not be to an external definition in the relocatable object file, but just an offset within that file.

5

Organized Variables

C has several methods for organizing variables of simple types (e.g., **int,float**). These include grouping of homogeneous variables (arrays), heterogeneous variables (structures) and overlapping variables (unions).

ARRAYS

Arrays in C work much the same as in other languages. They are groups of variables of the same type. Square brackets ([and]) are used to define and index arrays. The syntax for an array declaration is:

type variables-name[size];

The type is any type of variable described in Chapter 2. The **variable-name** follows the same roles as for simple variables. For example:

int iarr[5];

declares **iarr** to be an array of 5 integers. The individual elements in the array can be referenced as:

iarr[0]	first element
iarr[1]	second element
. . .	
iarr[4]	last element

Note that the index starts at 0 instead of 1. See Exhibit 5.1 for examples in other languages. If an array is an external or a **static** variable, it can be initialized in the declaration.

static int iarr[5] = {5,7,31,18,22};

initializes the elements to the values:

Element	Value
iarr[0]	5
iarr[1]	7

Exhibit 5.1 ARRAYS IN OTHER LANGUAGES

BASIC

DIM IARR(5)	definition
IARR(1)	reference
. . .	
IARR(5)	

FORTRAN

DIMENSION IARR(5)	definition
IARR(1)	reference
. . .	
IARR(5)	

PASCAL

VAR	
IARR: ARRAY[0..4] OF INTEGER;	definition
IARR[0]	reference
. . .	
IARR[4]	

PL/I

DECLARE IARR(0:4) FIXED BIN(15,0);	definition
IARR(0)	reference
. . .	
IARR(4)	

COBOL

01 TABLE-OF-INT	definition
05 IARR PICTURE 99999 OCCURS 5 TIMES.	
IARR(1)	reference
. . .	
IARR(5)	

Element	Value
iarr[2]	31
iarr[3]	18
iarr[4]	22

If an array is completely initialized, then its dimension does not need to be given. The compiler determines it from the number of initializing values. The above could be written as:

static int iarr[ ]={5,7,31,18,22};

Unlike some other languages, there are no operators in C that act on all elements of an array. To copy the values in one array to another, each element must be copied individually.

String constants

A string constant is the equivalent of a static array of characters terminated by the NUL ('\0') character. Unlike many other languages, strings in C do not include any count that is the length or number of characters in the string. Instead, the NUL character designates the end of the string.

A character array may be initialized using a string constant, rather than specifying the individual characters. For example:

```
static char carr[ ] = "ABCD";
```

is equivalent to:

```
static char carr[5] = {'A','B','C','D','\0'};
```

The '\0' is included in the second statement to match the terminating character of a string constant. The memory layout of **carr** is shown in Diagram 5.1.

Since static variables are set to 0 if they are not initialized, then:

```
static char darr[10] = "ABCDE";
```

is equivalent to:

```
static char darr[10] =
      {'A','B','C','D','E','\0',0,0,0,0};
```

If a string constant needs to be continued on more than one line of the source code, a backslash (\) followed by the carriage return is used to end the line to be continued. The constant continues with the first character of the next line.

Note that "" is the null string. It consists of just the terminating NUL character.

Multiply dimensioned arrays

Arrays can have more than one dimension. They are used much the same as in other languages. They are stored in memory such that the rightmost subscript varies the fastest.

```
int ia[6][5];
```

declares **ia** is to be an array of integers with two dimensions. Notice that the form is not **int ia[6,5]**, as in other languages. This would declare **ia** to be an array of **int** five long. (The comma is taken to be the comma operator, not a dimension separator). C treats multiply dimensioned arrays as multiple arrays of singly dimensioned arrays.

Diagram 5.1 MEMORY LAYOUT OF CARR

ELEMENT	ADDRESS	VALUE	ASCII VALUE IN MEMORY
carr[0]	1000	'A'	65
carr[1]	1001	'B'	66
carr[2]	1002	'C'	67
carr[3]	1003	'D'	68
carr[4]	1004	'\0'	0

Diagram 5.2 MEMORY LAYOUT OF IA

	ADDRESS	VALUE IN MEMORY
ia[0][0]	1000	1
ia[0][1]	1001	2
ia[0][2]	1002	3
ia[0][3]	1003	4
ia[0][4]	1005	5
ia[1][0]	1006	6
. . .		
ia[2][0]	1010	11
. . .		
ia[3][0]	1015	16
. . .		
ia[4][0]	1020	21
. . .		
ia[5][0]	1025	26
. . .		
ia[5][4]	1029	30

```
static int ia[6][5]={
    {1,2,3,4,5},
    {6,7,8,9,10},
    {11,12,13,14,15},
    {16,17,18,19,20},
    {21,22,23,24,25},
    {26,27,28,29,30}
};
```

initializes the array **ia** by rows. Diagram 5.2 shows how it would appear in memory. This yields:

Expression	Value
ia[2][3]	14
ia[5][0]	26

The extra pairs of braces are not necessary in the initializing portion. However if not all elements in a row are to be initialized, the braces force the compile to begin initializing the next row.

Arrays passed to functions

The name of an array can be used as an actual argument in a function call. The name is the equivalent of the address of the first element of the array. This means that the argument is being passed as a "call by reference" and that the called function can alter the values in the array in the calling routine. The corresponding formal parameter in the function may either be declared as a pointer (described in Chapter 6) or as an array.

If it is declared as an array, the leftmost dimension not need to be specified. For example, if **carr** as defined above was being passed to a function expecting a singly dimensioned array, then:

```
        func1d(arr1d)
        char arr1d[ ];
            {
            . . .
```

is sufficient to declare the parameter. For the doubly dimensioned array **ia**, then:

```
        func2d(arr2d)
        int arr2d[ ][5];
            {
            . . .
```

is sufficient. The function has no way of telling the actual size of an array being passed to it. If this is necessary, then either the array needs to contain some terminating element (such as '**\0**') or the size also needs to be an argument.

STRUCTURES

Structures are groups of variables. Unlike arrays, they can be composed of different types (i.e., integers and floats). They are comparable to records in other languages. Each structure can be treated as a whole or each element in the structure can be treated as a single variable.

To define a structure, one defines the elements in it:

```
        struct tag-type {
                variable declaration
                variable declaration
                    . . .
                }
        variable-name;
```

The *tag-type* is optional and will be discussed later. The *variable declarations* are the same as simple variable declarations. The *variable-name* follows the same rules as simple variable names. For example:

```
        struct {
                char month[10];
                int day;
                int year;
                }
        holiday;
```

declares **holiday** to be a structure which has three variables in it: a **char** array **month**, an **int day**, and an **int year**. See Exhibit 5.2 for the equivalents in other languages.

Member operator

Each member of the structure is the equivalent of a simple variable of its type. The member operator (**.**) is used to reference a member of a structure. For example:

Expression	References
holiday.month	a character array of length 10
holiday.month[0]	first character in **month**
holiday.day	an **int** variable
holiday.year	an **int** variable
holiday.day + +	increments **holiday.day** by 1
holiday.month[0] = 'C'	puts 'C' into the first element of **month**

Diagram 5.3 shows how the members of **holiday** are laid out in memory.

Tag-type

A structure may be given a *tag-type*. Once it is defined, it can be used to declare other structures with the same members. For example:

Exhibit 5.2 STRUCTURES IN OTHER LANGUAGES

BASIC

Nothing comparable

FORTRAN

Nothing comparable

PASCAL

```
TYPE                                               definition
    DATE = RECORD
            MONTH : ARRAY[0..9] OF CHAR;
            DAY : INTEGER;
            YEAR : INTEGER
    END;
VAR
    HOLIDAY : DATE;
    HOLIDAY.YEAR                               reference to element
```

PL/I

```
DECLARE 1 HOLIDAY,                                 definition
        5 MONTH CHAR(10),
        5 DAY   FIXED BIN(15,0),
        5 YEAR  FIXED BIN(15,0);
HOLIDAY.YEAR                                   reference to element
```

COBOL

```
01 HOLIDAY                                         definition
        05 MONTH PICTURE XXXXXXXXXX.
        05 DAY    PICTURE 99.
        05 YEAR   PICTURE 9999.
HOLIDAY.YEAR                                   reference to element
```

Diagram 5.3 LAYOUT OF HOLIDAY

MEMBER OF HOLIDAY	ADDRESS
month	500
day	510
year	512

```
struct date {
    char month[10];
    int day;
    int year;
    };
```

declares **date** to be a tag-type for a structure with three members in it: **month**, **day**, and **year**. Once **date** is defined this way, it can be used in other declarations.

```
struct date dayofyr;
```

declares **dayofyr** to be a structure variable of tag-type **date** with elements **dayofyr.month**, **dayofyr.day**, and **dayofyr.year**.

Tag-types for structures may be defined in the same declaration as that in which the structure variables are declared. For example:

```
struct date {
    char month[10];
    int day;
    int year;
    } dayofyr;
```

declares **date** as a tag-type and **dayofyr** to be a structure with that tag-type.

The only operation that can be performed on a structure as a whole is to take its address.

Expression	Value
&dayofyr	address of dayofyr
dayofyr/5	invalid

This means that structures cannot be passed to or returned from functions. A pointer to the structure must be passed. (See Chapter 6.) A structure cannot be copied into another structure by the assignment operator. It must be copied member by member.

The UNIX compiler does allow structures to be assigned and to be passed to and returned by functions.

sizeof

The compiler may place holes in the structure if memory alignment is necessary for the variable types. Some computers require that integers can only be placed in memory at even addresses. This may require that memory locations be skipped when laying out the structure. For example:

```
struct date1 {
    int day1;
    char month1[9];
```

```
    int year1;
    }
    birthday;
```

may have the locations shown on Diagram 5.4, if integers are required to be aligned on even addresses.

The actual length of a structure in bytes can be found by using the **sizeof** keyword. The compiler determines the actual size of the structure in bytes, including holes, and replaces **sizeof** by this value. The expression that **sizeof** operates on can be a variable name or the name of a data type.[1]

For example, for the structures outlined above:

Expression	Value
sizeof(holiday)	14
sizeof(birthday)	14
sizeof(struct date)	14
sizeof(struct date1)	14

Initialization of structures

Structure initialization looks much like array initialization. Only **static** or exernal structures can be initialized.

```
    static struct date holiday = {"JANUARY",1,1984}
```

or

```
    static struct date holiday =
        {{'J','A','N','U','A','R','Y','\0'},1,1984};
```

or

```
    static struct date holiday =
        {'J','A','N','U','A','R','Y','\0',0,0,1,1984};
```

causes **holiday** to have:

Expression	Value
holiday.month[4]	'A'
holiday.year	1984

The extra 0 values in the third initializer are required to make it the equivalent of the first two. If the zeros were not included, the last two characters of month would be set to 1 and 1984.[2] Diagram 5.5 gives the memory layout of **holiday**.

Diagram 5.4 LAYOUT OF BIRTHDAY

MEMBER OF BIRTHDAY	ADDRESS	SIZE IN BYTES
day1	600	2
month1	602	9
(hole)	611	1 byte for alignment
year1	612	2

Diagram 5.5 MEMORY LAYOUT OF HOLIDAY

VARIABLE	ADDRESS	VALUE
holiday.month[0]	1000	'J'
holiday.month[1]	1001	'A'
holiday.month[2]	1002	'N'
holiday.month[3]	1003	'U'
holiday.month[4]	1004	'A'
holiday.month[5]	1005	'R'
holiday.month[6]	1006	'Y'
holiday.month[7]	1007	'\0'
holiday.month[8]	1008	0
holiday.month[9]	1009	0
holiday.day	1010	1
holiday.year	1012	1984

Structures within structures

Structures can include structures as members. For example:

```
struct sc {
       int a;
       int b;
       };
struct {
       struct sc c;
       int d;
       } e;
```

has the following members:

Member reference	Type
e.c.a	int
e.c.b	int
e.d	int
e.c	structure of tag-type sc

Arrays of structures

There are also arrays of structures. For example:

```
struct date {
       char month[10];
       int day;
       int year;
       };
struct date somedays[10];
```

declares **somedays** to be an array of structures of tag-type **date**.

Expression   **References**

somedays[i].month[j]   the **j**th element in **month** in the **i**th element of **somedays**

somedays can be initialized by:

```
static struct date somedays[10]={
            {"JANUARY",10,1984},
            {"FEBRUARY",22,1984},
            . . .
            {"DECEMBER",25,1984}
            }
```

As with arrays, the inner braces and the array dimension are not necessary if all members and all elements are to be initialized. One could write:

```
static struct date somedays[ ]={
            "JANUARY",1,1984,
            "FEBRUARY",1,1984,
            . . .
            "DECEMBER",1,1984
            }
```

The expression **sizeof(somedays)/sizeof(struct date)** gives the number of elements in the array **somedays**.

Duplicate member names

The same member name may appear in two different structures if it has the same type in both structures and all preceding members of the two structures agree in type. This is because a member name represents an offset from the beginning of a structure. For example, it is permissible to do the following:

```
struct {
    int s;
    int t;
    char r;
    } one;
struct {
    int a;
```

Diagram 5.6 MEMORY LAYOUT OF MODEM

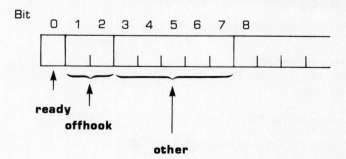

```
        int v;
        char r;
        } two;
```

In this example, **r** represents an offset of 4 bytes (the size of two **int**s) from the beginning of a structure. However, for ease of program maintenance, it is suggested that member names in structures be kept unique.[3]

Bit fields

A **struct** can contain fields of bits, rather than bytes. These fields are usually used to access machine-dependent values. Bit fields are an alternative to using bitwise operators to access individual bits in an integer. An example of a declaration for bit fields is:

```
        struct {
                unsigned int ready: 1;
                unsigned int offhook: 2;
                unsigned int other: 5;
                } modem;
```

This declares **modem** to be a structure of 8 bits with three members:

Member	Reference
modem.ready	first bit
modem.offhook	next two bits
modem.other	next five bits

These expressions may be used anywhere an **unsigned** integer may be used. **modem** will have the memory layout shown on Diagram 5.6 (assuming **int**s are required to align on even bytes and that bits in the sample machine are assigned left to right). Whether bit fields are laid out left to right or right to left is dependent on the computer.

Bit fields have a few limitations. A field cannot be wider than the size of an **int**. Fields must not overlap **int** boundaries. If one does, it will be aligned on the next integer boundary. The **&** address operator cannot be used on a field. A field that has a width of 0 forces the next field to be aligned on an integer boundary. A field that does not have a name may be used for padding. For example:

```
        struct {
                unsigned int wait    : 1;
                                     : 7;
                unsigned int stop    : 2;
                                     : 0;
                unsigned int conn    : 1;
                } comm;
```

causes **comm** to have members which are aligned according to Diagram 5.7.

UNIONS

A **union** allows the same storage locations to be referenced in more than one way. Usually this is done either to save space with static variables or to reference variables in machine dependent ways. The syntax for **union** is:

```
union tag-type {
    variable declaration;
    variable declaration;
    . . .
    }
    variable-name;
```

The *tag-type, variable declarations,* and *variable-name* follow the same pattern as for **struct.** An example is:

```
union {
    int i;
    float f;
    }
    u;
```

The size of a **union** is the size of the largest element in it. In the example, it would be four bytes long. The members of a union are designated in the same manner as members of structures.

Expression	Designates
u.i	the integer
u.f	the float

The members of a union are the equivalent of the simple types by which they are declared.

Expression	Notes
u.i = 5	The value 5 is put into the member **u.i**. If **u.f** is then referenced, its value will have changed.
u.f = 6.3	The value 6.3 is put into the member **u.f**. If **u.i** is then referenced, its value will have changed.

Diagram 5.8 shows how **u** might be laid out in memory. Exhibit 5.3 gives the equivalents in other languages.

Diagram 5.7 MEMORY LAYOUT OF COMM

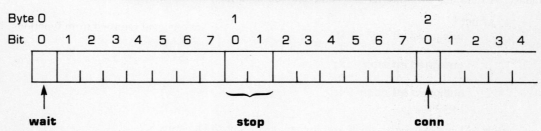

Diagram 5.8 LAYOUT OF UNION U

MEMBER OF U	ADDRESS	LENGTH
u.i	500	2
u.f	500	4

Exhibit 5.3 UNIONS IN OTHER LANGUAGES

BASIC

Nothing comparable

FORTRAN

```
INTEGER I
REAL F
EQUIVALENCE (I,F)
```

PASCAL

```
TYPE
       NUMTYPE = (FIXED,FLOAT);
       NUMBER = RECORD
       CASE NT : NUMTYPE OF
           FIXED  :
                    (I : INTEGER);
           FLOAT :
                    (F : REAL)
       END;
```

PL/I

```
DECLARE 1 ONEREC;
         5 I PICTURE '99999';
DECLARE 1 TWOREC DEFINED(ONEREC);
         5 F PICTURE '99V999';
```

COBOL

```
01 ONEREC
       05 I PICTURE 99999.
01 TWOREC REDEFINES ONEREC
       05 F PICTURE 99V999.
```

A **union** cannot be initialized. The only operation that can be performed on a **union** as a whole is to take its address. In UNIX C, **unions** can be assigned, passed to functions, and returned from functions, just as structures are.

The elements of **union**s can be **struct**s, arrays, or other **union**s, as well as simple variables. For example:

```
struct ss {
        int ia[5];
        char c;
        };
union   ua {
        struct ss s;
        float b;
        } us;
```

Diagram 5.9 LAYOUT OF US

VARIABLE	TYPE	ADDRESS	LENGTH
us	union	1000	15
us.s	structure	1000	11
us.s.ia	array	1000	10
us.s.ia[0]	integer	1000	2
us.s.ia[1]	integer	1002	2
us.s.ia[2]	integer	1004	2
us.s.ia[3]	integer	1006	2
us.s.ia[4]	integer	1008	2
us.s.c	character	1010	1
us.s.b	float	1011	4

Expression	Designates
us.s.ia[1]	second element in array
us.s.c	character
us.b	float

Diagram 5.9 gives the memory layout of **us**.

EXAMPLE FUNCTIONS

These are a few examples of routines using arrays and structures. More appear in the next chapter.

sumarr

This routine sums the elements in a floating point array. It returns the sum.

```
double sumarr(a,n)
/* sums a float array */
float a[ ]; /* array to be summed */
int n;     /* size of array */
  {
  double sum=0.0;
  int i;
  for (i=0;i<n;i++)
      {
      sum = sum + a[i];
      }
  return sum;
  }
```

invert

This routine inverts the sequence of numbers in an array. It uses double indexing and the comma operator in the **for** loop.

```
invert(a,num)
/* inverts the sequence of numbers in an array */
int a[ ]; /* array to be inverted */
int num; /* number of elements in array */
    {
    int i, j, temp;

    for (i = 0, j = num − 1;i<j;i + + , j − −)
        {
        temp = a[i];
        a[i] = a[ j];
        a[ j] = temp;
        }
    return 0;
    }
```

match

This routine compares a string against another string and returns the position (index) of a match, if any.

```
match(instr,mstr)
/* matches mstr against instr
        returns −1 or index of match */
char instr[ ]; /* String to be indexed into */
char mstr [ ]; /* String to be matched */
        {
        int ret;
        register int i, j,mcnt, ncnt;
        ncnt = strlen(instr);
        mcnt = strlen(mstr);
        ret = − 1;

        /* starting with each character */
        for (i = 0;i< = (ncnt − mcnt);i + +)
                {
                /* do the comparison against current string */
                for  (j = 0;j<mcnt;j + +)
                        {
                        if (mstr[j]! = instr[i + j]) break;
                        }
                /* if completed all loops, then a match */
                if  (j = = mcnt)
                        {
                        ret = i;
                        break;
                        }
                }
        return ret;
        }
```

midstr

The routine creates a substring of a string.

```
char *midstr(dest,string,start,length)
char dest[ ], string[ ];
int start, length;
    {
    int i,j;
    j=0;
    /* check to see if start is beyond string */
    if (start>strlen(string))
        {
        dest[0]='\0';
        }
    else
        {
        for (i=0;i<length;i++)
            {
            dest[i]=string[i+start];
            /* if at end of string, stop */
            if (string[i+start]=='\0') break;
            }
        dest[i]='\0';
        }
    return dest;
    }
```

atoint

This routine converts a string to an integer. It has a number of checks for a valid number. The return value is the integer which was converted or ERROR (-32767) if an error occurred.

```
atoint(str)
char str[ ];
/* converts an string to an integer
    range is -9999 to +9999.
    returns ERROR (-32767) if an error*/
    {
    int len;
    int ret=0;
    int sign=0;
    int cnt=0;
    int error=0;
    int i=0;
    int j;
    /* eliminate initial spaces */
    while (str[i]==' ')
        {
        i++;
        }
```

```
                /* check for a + or a - */
                if (str[i] = = '-')
                    {
                    sign = 1;
                    i + +;
                    }
                else if (str[i] = = '+')
                    {
                    i + +;
                    }
                for (j = 0;j<4;j + +)
                    {
                    /* check for a digit */
                    /* only accept 4 digits */
                    if (str[i] = = '\0') break;
                    if ((str[i]<'0') || (str[i]>'9'))
                        {
                        error = 1;
                        break;
                        }
                    /* found a digit, determine new value */
                    ret = ret*10 + (str[i] - '0');
                    i + +;
                    }
                /* if not at end of string, then error */
                if (str[i]! = '\0') error = 1;
                if (sign) ret = - ret;
                if (error) ret = - 32767;
                return ret;
                }
```

Structure example program

This program asks the user for a month, day, and a year. It compares the input to a table of stored dates and outputs whether the date is special (included in the table) or not.

```
        struct date {
                char month[10];
                int day;
                int year;
                };
        main ( )
        /* Determines if date is special */
                {
                int ret,i;
                struct date aday;

                static struct date special[ ] = {
                            {"October",25,1925},
                            {"November",4,1916},
```

```
                    {"October",8,1941},
                    {"March",29,1916},
                    {"February",27,1984}
                    };
        int size = sizeof (special)/sizeof (struct date);

        /* Input the date to be checked */
        printf("\nMonth? ");
        scanf("%10s",aday.month);
        printf("\nDay? ");
        scanf("%d",&aday.day);
        printf("\nYear? ");
        scanf("%d",&aday.year);

        /* Check it */
        ret = 0;
        for (i = 0;i<size;i + +)
                {
                if ( special[i].year = = aday.year
                    && special[i].day = = aday.day
                    && strcmp(special[i].month,
                    aday.month) = = 0 )
                    {
                    ret = 1;
                    break;
                    }
                }
        if (ret = = 0) printf("\n%s %d, %d is not special",
                aday.month,aday.day,aday.year);
        else printf("A special day!! %s %d %d",
                aday.month,aday.day,aday.year);
        exit(0);
        }
```

Footnotes

1. The **sizeof** operator can be applied to any expression or data type. For example, **sizeof(int)** is 2 for the typical machine, and **sizeof(birthday.month)** is 10. 2. The value 1984 will be truncated to a one-byte value. 3. Some compilers allow the use of the same member names even if they do not meet these requirements.

Pointers

A pointer variable contains the address of another variable. There are three main uses of pointers. First, they allow a function to change the values of the arguments in the calling routine. Second, they are used to designate areas of memory that have been dynamically allocated. Third, they make some array operations much faster.

POINTERS AND ADDRESSES

In C, a pointer is defined to point at one particular type of variable (e.g., an **int** or **float**). The C syntax for defining a variable as a pointer, rather than a regular variable, uses the asterisk (*****). This syntax is:

type *variable-name;

For example:

int *pj;	**pj** is a pointer variable that points at **int** variables
float *pq;	**pq** is a pointer variable that points at **float** variables

The address operator (**&**) applied to a variable yields the address of that variable.[1] For example:

```
int i=5;
int *pj;
. . .
pj=&i;
```

places the address of **i** into **pj**. Diagram 6.1 gives the memory layout for these variables.

Diagram 6.1 MEMORY LAYOUT FOR I AND PJ

Variable	Address	Value at address
i	874	5
pj	902	874

Exhibit 6.1 POINTERS IN OTHER LANGUAGES

BASIC

Nothing directly comparable. With PEEK(P) and POKE P, VALUE the variable P acts like an pointer variable to a **char** (one-byte) variable.

MBASIC

The VARPTR function acts likes the address operator (&).

FORTRAN

The EXTERNAL attribute acts like a pointer to a function.

PASCAL

```
TYPE
    N = RECORD
            I : INTEGER
            END;
    PK :  ↑N;
    . . .
    NEW(PK);
    PK ↑ .I = 5;
```

The POINTER type is a pointer variable. There is no address operator or function. The POINTER type only points to storage that is allocated dynamically by the NEW procedure.

PL/I

```
DECLARE I FIXED BIN(15,0) BASED (PK);
DECLARE PJ POINTER;
ALLOCATE I;
PK − >I=5;
```

The ADDR function acts like the address operator.

COBOL

Nothing comparable.

The contents of the address that a pointer contains is referenced by using the pointer operator (∗). Thus:

```
int i;
int ∗pj;
. . .
pj = &i;
∗pj = 5;
```

places the address of **i** into **pj**, then puts the value 5 into the address pointed at by **pj**, which is the address of **i**. Thus 5 goes into **i**. Pointers in other languages are shown in Exhibit 6.1.

A pointer variable with the pointer operator (∗) can be used anywhere a regular variable can be used. The following sets of instructions are equivalent:

```
int i=0;
int j=0;
j=i+1;
```

and

```
int i=0;
int j=0;
int *pk;
pk=&i;
j=*pk +1;
```

INITIALIZATION

Pointers can be initialized to the address of any external or static variable. Thus:

```
static int i;
int *pi=&i;
```

By convention, the value 0 is used for an invalid pointer (This is normally defined as **NULL** in a #define—see Chapter 7). **NULL** is usually returned by functions that return pointers to show that an error has occurred.

POINTERS AND ARRAYS

There is a close correspondence between pointers and arrays. The name of an array is equivalent to the address of the first element in the array. For example, given:

```
int iarr[5]={5,7,31,18,22};
int *ip;
```

then:

```
ip=&iarr[0];
```

is equivalent to:

```
ip=iarr;
```

Diagram 6.2 gives the memory layout for these variables.

The meaning of adding or subtracting an integer with a pointer is to add or subtract the memory size of the type of variable (**sizeof**) for which the pointer is declared. This is taken care of by the compiler. Since **ip** points at **int**s (which are two bytes long in the sample computer), then:

Expression	Value	Notes
ip	630	address of **iarr[0]**
*ip	5	value of 630
ip+1	632	address of **iarr[1]**
*(ip+1)	7	value at 632
*ip+1	6	value at 630 plus 1

Diagram 6.2 MEMORY LAYOUT OF IARR AND IP

Variable	Address	Value
iarr[0]	630	5
iarr[1]	632	7
iarr[2]	634	31
iarr[3]	636	18
iarr[4]	638	22
ip	802	630

Pointers and array indexing can be used almost interchangeably. An array name acts as a pointer constant. For example, with the above variables:

Expression	Value
iarr	5
iarr[0]	5
*(iarr)	5
iarr[1]	7
*(iarr + 1)	7

THIS IS THE ARRAY NAME → iarr

Note that **iarr[i]** and ***(iarr + i)** are equivalent. The compiler actually translates an indexed reference to an array to a pointer-type reference during the compilation process.

Since an array name is a constant, operations such as increment and decrement are not valid. However, an array name that is a formal parameter of a function is the equivalent of a pointer variable and can be used as such. When an address is passed to a function, it does not matter whether the function declares it as a pointer or an array. The sample code for **strlen** and **strcat** later in this chapter demonstrate this.

String constants

Because a string constant is the equivalent of a static array of **char**, then one can use the following:

```
char *pc = "ABC";
```

This sets up a static array in memory and initializes **pc** to point to it. See Diagram 6.3.

Diagram 6.3 MEMORY LAYOUT FOR PC

Variable	Address	Value
constant	731	'A'
constant	732	'B'
constant	733	'C'
constant	734	'\0'
pc	800	731

Arrays of pointers

There can be arrays of pointers. For example:

> static char *cp[3];

declares **cp** to be an array of three pointers to characters. Each of these could be initialized with a character string or other pointer value. For example:

> static char *cp[3] = {"XYZ","QRS","KLM"};

declares an array of three character pointers and initializes them to point to three string constants. See Diagram 6.4 to see how these are laid out in memory.

Doubly dimensioned arrays

Instead of using a double-dimensioned array, an array of pointers to arrays could be implemented. For example, with the doubly dimensioned array from Chapter 5 (**ia[6][5]**), one could use instead:

```
static int ia0[5] = {1,2,3,4,5};
static int ia1[5] = {6,7,8,9,10};
static int ia2[5] = {11,12,13,14,15};
static int ia3[5] = {16,17,18,19,20,};
static int ia4[5] = {21,22,23,24,25};
static int ia5[5] = {26,27,28,29,30};
static int *pia[6] = {ia0,ia1,ia2,ia3,ia4,ia5};
```

then **pia[i][j]** or ***(pia[i]+j)** gives the **j**th element from the **i**th array. Using this is quicker than the

Diagram 6.4 MEMORY LAYOUT FOR CP

Variable	Address	Value
constant	731	'X'
constant	732	'Y'
constant	733	'Z'
constant	734	'\0'
constant	735	'Q'
constant	736	'R'
constant	737	'S'
constant	738	'\0'
constant	739	'K'
constant	740	'L'
constant	741	'M'
constant	742	'\0'
cp[0]	900	731
cp[1]	902	735
cp[2]	904	739

Diagram 6.5 MEMORY LAYOUT FOR IA AND IARR

Variable	Address	Value
ia0[0]	1000	1
ia0[1]	1001	2
ia0[2]	1002	3
ia0[3]	1003	4
ia0[4]	1004	5
ia1[0]	1005	6
ia2[0]	1010	11
ia3[0]	1015	16
ia4[0]	1020	21
ia5[0]	1025	26
ia5[4]	1029	30
pia[0]	2000	1000
pia[1]	2002	1005
pia[2]	2004	1010
pia[5]	2010	1025

computation required for a second dimension. However it does require more storage for the array of pointers. Diagram 6.5 shows the memory layout for these arrays.

POINTER ARITHMETIC

There are only a few operations one should perform with the value of a pointer. These operations affect the address that the pointer is pointing to, not the value at that address. These operations are assigning the value to another pointer, adding and subtracting an integer, and comparing for equality to another pointer value. Pointers can be added and subtracted from each other. However, the only meaningful results of pointer arithmetic arise when the two pointers point at different elements of the same array. For example: Given:

```
static int iarr[10];
int *ip = &iarr[0];
int *iq = &iarr[4];
```

then:

Expresson	Value	Notes
iq − ip	4	There are 4 elements of type **int** between **iq** and **ip**

Note that although C allows pointers to be used just like integers, any usage other than that mentioned will make the routines nonportable.

POINTERS AND STRUCTURES

Pointers to structures are defined in a similar manner to pointers to other variables. For example, given:

```
struct date {
        char month[10];
        int day;
        int year;
        };
```

then

```
struct date *pntdate:
```

declares **pntdate** to be a pointer to structures with tag-type of **date**. If:

```
pntdate = &birthday;
```

then one can refer to:

Expression	References
(*pntdate).month[4]	birthday.month[4]
(*pntdate).year	birthday.year

A shorthand notation can be used for the (*...). This is the —> operator. It is used to refer to a member of a structure using a pointer to that structure. For example, the above references could be stated as:

Expression	References
pntdate—>month[4]	birthday.month[4]
pntdate—>year	birthday.year

Pointers can be used to index through arrays of structures. If:

```
struct date holidays[12];
        . . .
struct date *pnthldy;
```

and

```
*pnthldy = &holidays[0]
```

or, equivalently:

```
*pnthldy = holidays;
```

then

Expression	References
pnthldy—>year	year of holiday[0]
(pnthldy + 5)—>day	day of holiday[5]
pnthldy + +	address of holiday[1]

Diagram 6.6 DOUBLE-LINKED LIST

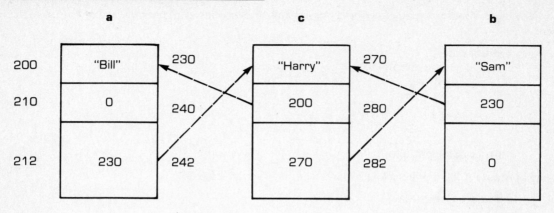

A pointer points at a particular data type. If it is necessary to assign a value that points at another data type, the cast operator should be used. For example, given:

```
char *cp;
struct date *cp;
```

then:

```
dp = (struct date *) cp;
```

converts the type of pointer value from a **char** pointer to a **struct date** pointer. This operation does not guarantee proper alignment of structure members. The program must check that. Many compilers do not require that this cast be used, so

```
dp = cp;
```

will be accepted. Note that with:

```
dp = (struct date *) cp + 1;
```

the 1 increments the value by the **sizeof** of **date** and not of a **char**.

Pointers to structures within structures

A structure may contain a pointer to structures of its tag-type within itself. For example:

```
struct link {
      char word [10]
      struct link *left;
      struct link *right;
      }
```

declares that **link** is a tag-type that contains a character array word, and two pointers that point to structures with tag-type **link**. If **link** was declared as above, then the following could be coded:

```
static struct link a={"BILL",0,&c};
static struct link b={"SAM",&c,0};
static struct link c={"HARRY",&a,&b};
```

This would look like Diagram 6.6. This is called a doubly linked list. A example program using a linked list is in Appendix A.

Pointers to **union**s follow the same rules as pointers to structures.

POINTERS AND FUNCTIONS

C uses "call by value" to pass single-valued arguments to functions. This means that the values of the arguments in the calling function are passed to the called function. The called function cannot directly alter the value of variables in the calling function. If this operation is required, one can use the C equivalent of "call by reference." To do this, the calling function passes the addresses of variables, instead of their values. For example:

```
int a=5;
int b=7;
func(&a,b);
```

will pass the value of the address of **a** and the value 7. **func** should define the formal parameters to be a pointer and a value by the following:

```
func(q,r)
int *q,r;
```

When **func** is called, the memory used by the routines will look like Diagram 6.7. If in **func**, there is an assignment:

```
*q=20;
```

then on return from **func**, **a** in the calling routine will have the value 20. Note that **q**=**20** is also a valid assignment. It would have the result that the value of **q** would be changed to 20. Later on, if there was an assignment *q=5, then the value at memory location 20 would be changed to 5.

When a function expects a pointer value as an argument, the calling routine can use the name of an array or the value of an address operator applied to a simple variable. If a structure pointer is being passed, the address operator must be used on the name of the structure.

Diagram 6.7 MEMORY LAYOUT FOR CALL BY REFERENCE

IN CALLING ROUTINE:			IN FUNC	
Variable	Address	Value at address	Expression	Value
a	764	5	q	764
b	766	7	r	7
			*q	5

Functions returning pointers

A function can return a pointer to a structure. This is commonly used in the input/output routines where the open functions return pointers to structures of type **FILE**. (See Chapter 8.)

```
struct date *func(a)
int a;
    {
    . . .
    }
```

is the definition of a function that returns a pointer to a structure with tag-type **date**.

```
struct date *func( );
```

declares within a routine that calls **func** that it is a function that will return a pointer to a structure with tag-type **date**.

The UNIX compiler permits functions to return a structure, not just a pointer to a structure.

Pointers to functions

Since the name of a function is equivalent to its address, it is possible to have pointers to functions. The coding starts to get a bit tricky, but it may be a useful feature to use.

```
int (*fp)( )
```

declares **fp** to be a pointer to a function returning an integer. (Note that **int *fp( )** declares **fp** to be a function that returns a pointer to an **int**.) Given this declaration, then

Expression	Notes
int func( );	declares **func** to be a function returning an **int**
fp=func;	address of **func** into **fp**
(*fp) (parm);	calls the function whose address is in **fp** (this is **func**), passing it the value of **parm**.

This feature is used with the **qsort** routine which is supplied with many compilers. **qsort** is a general purpose sorting routine that has the parameters:

```
qsort(arr,size,number,compare)
char *arr;
int size;
int number;
int (*compare)( );
```

arr points at the array to be sorted. Each element in **arr** is **size** bytes. The array is **number** elements long. **compare**( ) is a pointer to a function supplied by the calling program. This function must return a 1, 0, or −1 (for <, =, or >), depending on the comparison of two elements passed to it.

Note that a pointer to a function cannot be manipulated as pointers to other data types because there is no size associated with a function pointer.

One can have arrays of pointers to functions. For example:

```
int (*fp[8])( )
```
declares **fp** to be an array of pointers to functions

int func ( );	declares **func** to be a function

. . .

fp[5] = func;	address of **func** into 6th element of **fp**
(*fp[5])(parm);	calls the function whose address is in 6th element of **fp**, passing it the value of **parm**

COMPLICATED TYPES

A declaration can be made almost infinitely complex. Except in very rare cases, it is better to keep them more simple than the following:

> struct quid ***q[3];

declares **q** to be an array of three pointers that point to pointers that point to pointers that point to structures of tag-type **quid**.

> struct day *(*q[3])( )

declares **day** to be an array of three pointers to functions that return pointers that point to structures of tag-type **day**. Diagram 6.8 gives a the memory layout for the variable **q**.

EXAMPLE FUNCTIONS

There are some example routines that use pointers. The first four are rewrites using pointers of routines that were introduced in the last chapter.

Diagram 6.8 MEMORY LAYOUT FOR Q

IF

q[0] = func1;
q[1] = func2;
q[2] = func3;

AND

Address	Reference
	q[0]
892	
1089	start of code for **func1**
1532	start of code for **func2**
1783	start of code for **func3**

THEN

Variable	Address	Value
q[0]	892	1089
q[1]	894	1532
q[2]	896	1783

sumarr

This routine sums the elements in an floating point array. It returns the sum.

```
double sumarr (a,n)
/* sums a float array */
float *a; /* array to be summed */
int n;   /* size of array */
  {
  double sum=0.0;
  while (n--)
      {
      sum += *(a++);
      }
  return sum;
  }
```

match

This routine compares a string against another string and returns the position (index) of a match, if any.

```
match(instr,mstr)
/* matches mstr against instr
      returns -1 or index of match */
char *instr; /* String to be indexed into */
char *mstr; /* String to be matched */
      {
      int ret;
      register int i, j, mcnt, ncnt, k;
      char *mpnt,*npnt;
      ncnt=strlen(instr);
      mcnt=strlen(mstr);
      npnt=instr;
      ret=-1;
      i=0;
      k=ncnt-mcnt+1;
      /* starting with each character */
      while (k--)
          {
          npnt=instr++;
          mpnt=mstr;
          j=mcnt;
          /* do the comparison against current instr */
          while ( (*(mpnt++)==*(npnt++)) && (j--) )
              {
              ;
              }
          /* if j is 0, then match was found */
          if (j==0)
              {
              ret=i;
```

```
                              break;
                           }
                  i++;
               }
          return ret;
       }
```

midstr

This routine creates a substring of a string.

```
        midstr(dest,string,start,length)
        /* creates substring of a stirng */
        char *dest;   /* destination of substring */
        char *string; /* string to use */
        int start;       /* starting character (0==first) */
        int length;    /* length of substring */
           {
        if (start<strlen(string))
              {
              string = string + start;
              while ( (length − −) && (*string! = '\0') )
                    {
                    *dest + + = *string + +;
                    }
              }
           *dest = '\0';
           return 0;
           }
```

atoint

This routine converts a string to an integer. It has a number of checks for a valid number. The return value is the integer that was converted or ERROR (−32767) if an error occurred.

```
        atoint(str)
        char *str;
        /* converts an string to an integer
              range is −9999 to +9999.
              returns ERROR (−32768) if an error */
              {
        int len;
        int ret=0;
        int sign=0;
        int cnt=0;
        int error=0;
        len = strlen(str);
        /* eliminate initial spaces */
        while (*str = = ' ')
                {
                len − −;
```

```
            str++;
            }
/* check for a '+' or a '-'*/
if (*str=='-')
            {
            sign=1;
            len--;
            str++;
            }
else if (*str=='+')
            {
            str++;
            len--;
            }
while (len--)
            {
            /* check for a digit */
            /* only accept 4 digits */
            if ((*str<'0') || (*str>'9') || (cnt==4))
                {
                error=1;
                break;
                }
            /* found a digit, determine new value */
            ret=ret*10+(*(str++)-'0');
            cnt++;
            }
if (sign) ret=-ret;
if (error) ret=-32767;
return ret;
}
```

transpos

This routine transposes a square matrix.

```
transpos(iarr,m)
/* transposes square matrix of size m*/
int *iarr; /* array to transpose */
int m;     /* size of array */
            {
            int temp,*p1,*p2;
            int i,j;
            int last;
            /* each row */
            for (i=0;i<m;i++)
                    {
                    /* each column */
                    for (j=i+1;j<m;j++)
```

```
                    {
                    p1 = iarr + (i*m) + j;
                    p2 = iarr + (j*m) + i;
                    temp = *p1;
                    *p1 = *p2;
                    *p2 = temp;
                    }
            }
        return;
        }
```

Program using structures

This program inputs a date and determines whether it is one of a list of dates that is stored in a table. The program uses a subroutine to demonstrate pointers to structures.

chkdate

```
        struct date {
                char month[10];
                int day;
                int year;
                };
        main( )
        /* determines if date is special */
                {
                int ret;
                struct date aday;
                printf("\nMonth? ");
                scanf("%10s",aday.month);
                printf("\nDay? ");
                scanf("%d",&aday.day);
                printf("\nYear? ");
                scanf("%d",&aday.year);
                ret = spday(&aday);
                if (ret = = 0) printf("\n%s %d, %d is not special",
                    aday.month,aday.day,aday.year);
                else prinf("A special day!! %s %d %d",
                    aday.month,aday.day,aday.year);
                exit(0);
                }
        spday(someday)
        /* determines if day is a special day */
        struct date *someday; /* pointer to date to match */
                {
                static struct date special[ ] =
                    {
                    {"October",25,1925},
                    {"November",4,1916},
```

```
            {"October",8,1941},
            {"March",29,1916},
            {"February",27,1984}
            };
        int size = sizeof(special)/sizeof(struct date);
        int i;
        int sp = 0;
        for (i = 0;i<size;i + +)
            {
            if ( special[i].year = = someday - >year
                && special[i].day = = someday - >day
                && strcmp(special[i].month, someday - >month) = = 0 )
                {
                sp = 1;
                break;
                }
            }
    return sp;
    }
```

Setmem

This routine sets a number of memory locations to a given value.

```
    setmem(address,number,towhat)
    /* sets memory locations to a given value */
    char *address; /* address to start */
    int number;       /* number of bytes to set */
    char towhat;      /* byte to set addresses to */
        {
        while (number - -)
            {
            *(address + +) = towhat;
            }
        return 0;
        }
```

Current disk drive

On many microcomputer operating systems, the identity of the currently logged disk drive is kept in an absolute location in memory. If this were kept in one byte at memory location 72, then a function might look like:

```
    curdsk( )
    /* returns currently logged disk drive */
        {
        char *pdrive = 72; /* 72 is absolute location */
        return *pdrive;
        }
```

Note that applications such as this are computer and operating system dependent.

Memory-mapped screen output

On many systems, the output screen for the terminal is kept in computer memory. This is called "memory-mapped screen output." The screen could be accessed by using an array of character pointers. For example:

```
static char *lines[ ]={0X4000,0X4040,0X4080...};
```

The absolute values shown in the initialization should correspond to the addresses of the first character in each line of the screen. A character can then be placed at a row and column by simply:

```
lines[row][column]=chr;
```

Sample character functions from the C library

To illustrate pointers and arrays, the following examples are possible implementations of library functions that are supplied with many compilers.

strlen

strlen computes the length of a string. Its parameter is a pointer to a character string. The return value is the length of the string, not including the terminating null character. This could be written as:

```
strlen(instr)
char instr[ ];
    {
    register int i=0;
    while (instr[i]!='\0')
        {
        i++;
        }
    return i;
    }
```

or, using pointers:

```
strlen(instr)
char *instr;
    {
    register int i=0;
    while (*(instr++)!='\0')
        {
        i++;
        }
    return i;
    }
```

or getting concise and eliminating the test against 0:

```
strlen(instr)
char *instr;
    {
```

```
              register int i=0;
              while (*instr++)
                    {
                    i++;
                    }
              return i;
              }
```

or, using pointer arithmetic;

```
         strlen(instr)
         char *instr;
              {
              char *cp;
              cp=instr;
              while (*cp)
                    {
                    cp++;
                    }
              return (cp−instr);
              }
```

In calling **strlen**, one needs to pass it a character pointer. Given:

```
         char *cp="ABC";
         static char ca[3]={'A','B','\0'};
         static char cb[ ]="ABCD";
         char *cc=ca;
```

then:

Expression	Value
strlen(cp)	3
strlen(ca)	2
strlen(&ca[0])	2
strlen(cb)	4
strlen(&cb[2])	2
strlen(cc)	2

strcat

strcat concatenates two strings. Its parameters are two pointers to character strings. The first is the destination string and the second is the string to concatenate. The return value is the first character pointer. The destination needs to be long enough to hold the concatenated string. One possible coding is:

```
         char *strcat(dest,in)
            char dest[ ],in[ ];
                 {
                 int i=0,j=0;
                 while (dest[i]!='\0')
```

```
                        {
                        i+ +;
                        }
                while ((dest[i+ +] = in[j+ +])! = '\0')
                        {
                        ;
                        }
                return dest;
                }
```

or

```
        char *strcat(dest,in)
        char *dest,*in;
                {
                char *save;
                save = dest;
                while (*(dest+ +)! = '\0')
                        {
                        ;
                        }
                dest− −;
                while ((*(dest+ +) = *(in+ +))! = '\0')
                        {
                        ;
                        }
                return save;
                }
```

For example, given:

```
        char *cp = "ABC";
        static char ca[10] = {'A','B','\0'};
        static char cb[ ] = "ABCD";
        char *cc = cb;
```

then:

Expression	Result
strcat(ca,cb)	ca = "ABABCD"
strcat(ca,cp)	ca = "ABABC"
strcat(ca,cc)	ca = "ABABCD"

Footnote

1. It cannot be used with register variables or bit fields.

7

The Preprocessor and Other Compiler Features

Compilers include a preprocessor that expands macro definitions, a method for defining data types, recursive functions, and command line argument passing. Each of these aspects will be discussed separately.

PREPROCESSOR

C language compilers include a preprocessor front end. This translates the input source code to the form that the compiler actually sees. There are several instructions that can be given to the preprocessor. The most common are the **#define** and the **#include**.

#define

The **#define** form is the equivalent of the macro substitution found in many assembly languages. It looks like:

#define *NAME xxxxx*

where *NAME* is the symbol to be replaced and *xxxxx* is any string of characters. It may continue onto more lines by putting a backslash (\) at the end of each line to be continued. The substitution is made throughout the source code. There is no semicolon (;) at the end of the **#define**. If a semicolon appeared, it would become part of the replacement. A **#define** must appear in the source code ahead of its use. For example, if:

#define TRUE 1

then:

if (TRUE) . . .

is translated by the preprocessor to

if (1) . . .

The **#define** can take arguments. These are given directly after the name:

#define *NAME***(***arg1,arg2...***)** *xxxxx*

Given:

#define PLUSONE(x) x + 1

then:

PLUSONE(y)

is translated to:

y + 1

The **#define** is commonly used in place of any value that might need changing. In a well-designed program, numbers may never appear in the source code outside of **#define** statements.

#defines can reference previous **#define**s. For example:

#define ONE 1
#define TWO ONE + ONE

will replace **ONE** by **1** and **TWO** by **1 + 1** wherever they appear.

Macros versus functions

A typical use of a **#define** is to make what appears to be a function call into in-line code. A typical example is taking the maximum of two numbers. A function **max** might be defined as:

```
max(x,y)
int x,y;
/* returns max of the two inputs */
    {
    return ( x>y ? x : y);
    }
```

Instead of using the function as defined above, one could instead include in the calling routine the macro:

#define max(a,b) (a>b ? a : b)

This would have the effect of replacing each call to **max** by the conditional expression. Using the macro instead of a function call may result in faster execution, but will use more memory.

The macro definition is frequently used in the standard subroutine library. For example:

#define getchar( ) getc(stdin)

Appendix D lists the operations of these input functions. This **#define** is usually included in **stdio.h**. **#define** can be any character string. Thus the following might be used:

```
#define READY modem&0x80
#define OFFHOOK modem&0x60
#define OTHER modem&0x1F
int modem;
```

READY represents the equivalent of the left-most bit of **modem**. **OFFHOOK** represents the next two bits of **modem**. **OTHER** is the next five bits. Diagram 5.6 gives the layout of **modem**. Definitions of this type can be used with compilers that do not support the bit fields of structures.

The preprocessor allows a name to be redefined. For example:

```
#define ONE 1
    . . .
#define ONE 2
```

Any use of **ONE** between the two definitions will have the replacement value of **1**. Any use of **ONE** after the second definition will have the replacement value of **2**. The use of this feature is not suggested except in very rare cases because it makes code maintenance difficult.

#include

The **#include** instruction includes another source file into the current one for the purposes of compilation. The **#include** takes two forms:

```
#include "filename"
#include <filename>
```

The first one includes the file named *filename* as it is found on the current section of a system (such as a user's section). The latter one includes the file named *filename* from some standard system-dependent place (e.g., a master disk section).

Include files usually are listings of program-wide **#define**s and **extern** files. Compilers usually have one standard **#include** file. This is **stdio.h** for standard input/output definitions. Definitions for **NULL** (for pointers) and **EOF** (for file input) are found in this file.

Include files can be nested within each other. That is, an included file can contain **#include** statements. Each compiler has its own limit as to the number of files that may be nested in this way.

Other preprocessor statements

There are several more preprocessor statements supported by C. These permit conditional compilation of code segments to be determined by the pre-compile phase. That is, some of the code may be either treated as comments and not processed by the compiler or treated as code to be compiled, depending on a compile time test.

#undef *name*	removes a #define definition so *name* becomes undefined
#if *exp*	tests to see if constant integer expression *exp* is non-zero
#ifdef *name*	tests to see if the *name* is defined by a **#define**
#ifndef *name*	tests to see if the *name* is currently undefined (has never been **#define**d or has been **#undef**ined)

If the result of these **if** tests are true, then the suceeding lines are compiled until an **#else** or **#endif** is encountered. Otherwise, the lines following the **#else** to the **#endif** are compiled.

#else	signals the start of the lines to be compiled if the **if** test was false
#endif	end of the **if** statement. Allows **if** statements to be nested.

For example, the following allows different codes to be compiled based on the definition of **COMPUTER**.

```
#define Z80 1
#define M6502 2
#define COMPUTER M6502
       /* this definition must change
           for each computer */
#if COMPUTER = = Z80
       /* Z80 code */
    . . .
#else
#if COMPUTER = = M6502

    /* 6502 code */
    . . .
#endif
#endif
```

One additional preprocessor statement is used mainly by programs which create C programs. This is the **#line** statement.

#line *constant*   used to tell the C compiler a line number for the purposes of printing messages.

TYPEDEFS

A **typedef** does not define a new type of variable. It provides a simple way of hiding the actual structure from a program. This allows the program to be more portable. For example:

typedef int SIZE;

declares **SIZE** to be a type that can be used in declarations and elsewhere.

SIZE i,j;

declares **i** and **j** to be of **typedef SIZE**, which has been defined as **int**. If the maximum values that might be stored in these increase at some future date, then simply changing the typedef to

typedef long int SIZE;

and recompiling will change the declarations of variables declared as **SIZE** throughout the program.

typedefs are almost the equivalent of **#defines**. For example:

**#define SIZE long int
SIZE i,j;**

has the same effect as the above **typedef**. However, **typedef**s can handle complicated types more easily than **#defines**. For example:

**typedef int ∗PNTARR[10]
PNTARR pj;**

and

**#define PNTARR1(x) int ∗x[10]
PNTARR1(pj);**

both declare **pj** to be an array of 10 pointers to **int**. The **typedef** looks like a regular declaration while the **#defines** looks like a function call.

The **typedef** is somewhat neater. The **typedef** is usually used in defining the structure of a file pointer. A typical example of a **FILE** definition that a compiler might include in its **stdio.h** file is:

```
typedef struct {
        char *buffer; /* pointer to file buffer */
        int mode;       /* file access mode */
        int bufpnt;     /* index into file buffer */
        int filenum;    /* file number */
        } FILE;
```

EXPRESSION EVALUATION

Constant expressions can be used for initializing static and external variables, for **case** labels in **switch** constructs, and as the size of arrays. These expressions are made up of integer or character constants that may be combined by arithmetic, bitwise, relational, or conditional operators. The **sizeof** operator with a variable or tag-type may be used as a constant. The addresses of static and external variables may also be used as constants. Constant expressions are evaluated at compile time, rather than execution time. For example:

Expression	Notes
#define SIZE 7	
static char a[SIZE + 2];	**a** is size 9
int b = sizeof(a);	**b** initialized to 9
char *pnt = a;	**pnt** initialized to address of **a**

RECURSION

The C language supports recursive routines. A recursive routine can call itself. Most recursive algorithms can be written in a non-recursive manner. However recursion is sometimes cleaner. The Flowchart 7.1 gives an example of a non-recursive routine that calculates factorials. A recursive routine that does the same thing is shown in Flowchart 7.2.

The non-recursive routine might look like:

```
factor(i)
/* computes factorial */
int i; /* number to compute factorial for */
    {
    int prod;
    if (i = = 0) prod = 0;
    else
        {
        prod = i;
        while ( - - i > 0)
        {
```

Flowchart 7.1 NONRECURSIVE ROUTINE

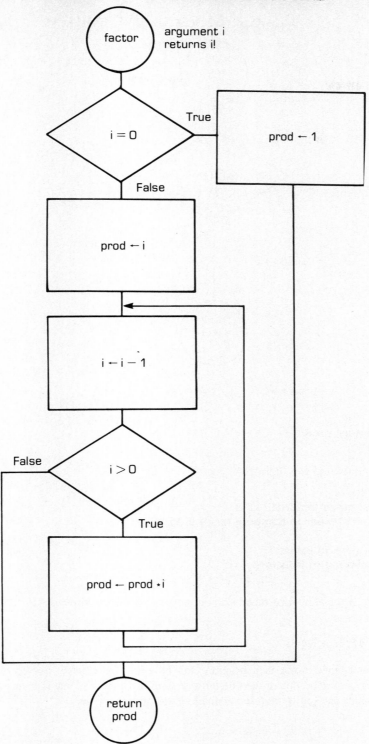

Flowchart 7.2 RECURSIVE ROUTINE

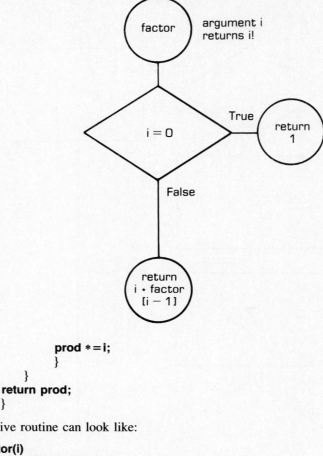

```
            prod *= i;
            }
        }
    return prod;
    }
```

The recursive routine can look like:

```
factor(i)
/* computes factorial */
int i; /* number to compute factorial for */
    {
    if (i==0) return 1;
    else return i*factor(i-1);
    }
```

The memory management of recursive routines is covered in Appendix F.

MAIN PROGRAM

The function labeled **main** in a program can have two parameters passed to it. These values are determined by the command line of the operating system (i.e., the line that is entered to get the program to run). This parameter passing to *main* is available under most systems.

The two parameters passed are an argument count and an array of pointers to arguments that are character strings. For example, if the program **help** is executed by typing the instruction to the operating system:

help editing

the two parameter values that are passed to the program are:

Parameter	Value
first	2
second	array of two addresses first points to ''help'' second points to ''editing''

If the program looks like:

```
HELP
main(argc,argv)
int argc;
char *argv[ ];
    {
    if (argc<2)
        {
        printf("no help requested");
        exit(2);
        }
    mkupper(argv[1]);
    if (!strcmp(argv[1],"EDITING"))
        {
        printf("here is help for editing");
        /* help for editing */
        }
    else if (!strcmp(argv[1],"PRINTING"))
        {
        printf("help is help for printing");
        /* help for printing */
        }
    /* checks for any other help */
    else
        {
        printf("no help for %s available",argv[1]);
        exit(1);
        }
    exit(0);
    }
mkupper(string)
/* Makes a string all upper case */
char *string;
    {
    int i;
    i=strlen(string);
    while (i--)
```

```
        {
        *string = toupper(*string);
        string + + ;
        }
    return;
    }
```

it will print out:

here is help for editing

A common convention in passing values to a program is to use the hyphen (-) to prefix a flag or option. For example:

help -f editing

might give "full" help. Usually the flags are given before the name of any files or other similar items. A **main** program that interprets options might look something like:

```
#define TRUE 1
#define FALSE 0
main(argc,argv)
int argc;
char *argv[ ];
    {
    int full;
    register int i;
    char flag;
    full = FALSE;

    if (argc = = 1) {
        printf("No help specified");
        exit(2);
        }
    for (i = 1;i<argc;i + +)
        {
        if (*argv[i] = = ' - ')
            {
            /* this is a flag */
            flag = toupper(*(argv[i] + 1));
            if (flag = = 'F') full = TRUE;
            else
                {
                printf("\nbad option %c",flag);
                exit(1);
                }
            }
        else
            {
```

```
                    /* this is the request */
                    if (i!=argc-1)
                       {
                       printf("too many arguments or wrong order");
                       exit(2);
                       }
                    mkupper(argv[i]);
                    if (!strcmp(argv[i],"EDITING"))
                       {
                       if (full)
                          {
                          printf("\nfull help for editing");
                          /* print full help for editing */
                          }
                       else
                          {
                          printf("\nhere is some editing help");
                          }
                       }
                    else if (!strcmp(argv[i],"PRINTING"))
                       {
                       if (full)
                          {
                          printf("\nfull help for printing");
                          }
                       else
                          {
                          printf("\nhere is some printing help");
                          /* print help for printing */
                          }
                       }
                    /* checks for anything else */
                    else
                       {
                       printf("no help for %s",argv[i]);
                       exit(1);
                       }
                    } /* end of else for non-dash */
                 } /* end of for loop */
          exit(0);
          }
mkupper(string)
/* Makes a string all upper case */
char *string;
          {
          int i;
          i=strlen(string);
          while (i--)
```

```
        {
        *string = toupper (*string);
        string + + ;
        }
    return;
    }
```

A compiler supplied routine (sometimes called _ **main ( )**) is usually the first routine called from the operating system when a program starts execution. This routine sets up any file redirection, opens the standard input and output files, and passes the parameter list from the command line to the programmer-written routine called **main**. (See Chapter 8 for information about files.)

exit

A function supplied with C compilers is **exit( )**. This function closes all open files and returns a value to the operating system. This value is used by some operating systems to determine whether to continue with processing a series of commands or to abort the series. **exit** can be called by any routine. If the routine labeled **main( )** finishes without explicitly calling **exit**, it is implicitly called.

exit(5);   returns to the operating system a value of 5

Structured programming suggests that **exit** should only be called by the **main** program or by a fatal-error handling routine. Spreading calls to **exit** throughout several routines increases the time required to understand the program code.

ENUMERATION

The UNIX compiler has an additional data type called the enumerated type. This data type can be found in other languages such as Pascal. A variable of an enumerated data type can only take on the values declared for that type. The syntax of a **enum**-type declaration is:

enum tag-type {*enum1,enum2*....};

The *enum1, enum2*.... are identifiers that represent the possible values of the tag-type. For example:

enum days {monday,tuesday,wednesday,
thursday,friday,saturday,sunday};

specifies that **days** is a **tag-type** for an **enum**-type variable, which can only take on the values of **monday . . .** through **sunday**.

If **days** was declared as above, then

enum days day;

declares **day** to be an **enum**-type variable that can only take on the values **monday...sunday**.

Enumeration types are represented internally by integers. The first identifier is given the value of 0, the next of 1, and so forth. Thus for the above:

Identifier	Value
monday	0
tuesday	1
wednesday	2
thursday	3
friday	4
saturday	5
sunday	6

An enumeration identifier is normally used with variables of the enumeration type. For example, with **days** and **day** above:

Expression	Value
day = = monday	1 if day is monday, 0 otherwise
day>friday	1 if day is saturday or sunday, 0 otherwise

Some C compilers currently do not strictly enforce this typing. So the following is possible. Given:

```
int inday;
```

then

Expression	Value
inday = = monday	1 if **inday** had value of 1, 0 otherwise
3 + tuesday	4

If **day** has the value **wednesday**, then **day + +** has the value of 3.

Values differing from the default values can be assigned to the enumeration identifiers. This is specified by giving the constant after the identifier. For example:

```
enum weekend {saturday = 6,sunday};
```

yields:

Identifier	Value
saturday	6
sunday	7

Also,

```
enum openday {monday = 1,wednesday = 3,friday = 5}
```

yields:

Identifier	Value
monday	1
wednesday	3
friday	5

8

Input/Output

The C language does not directly provide any input or output. Instead, a standard library of input/output (I/O) functions is provided with most compilers. These functions provide many of the same operations as I/O statements in other languages. They include character and formatted I/O with the terminal and with disk files. The routines usually come in two versions—buffered and unbuffered. Buffered routines use input or output buffers that allow a program to read or write as little as a character at a time. Unbuffered routines directly access devices.

The full list of options for each standard library routine are given in Appendix D. A brief summary of the main routines is given here.

FILES

Three files are implicitly present in C programs. These are the standard input (**stdin**), standard output, (**stdout**), and standard error (**stderr**). Unless otherwise specified, **stdin** is assumed to be the keyboard of the terminal that is running the program, and **stdout** and **stderr** are the screen (or paper, on a teletype) of the terminal. These may be redirected to other places, as will be described in the section on pipes and filters.

In inputting from a file, there is always the possibility that no data will be available. This case is usually handled by the input function returning the value **EOF**. This is a **#define** that is included in a compiler's **stdio.h** file. Its replacement value is usually −1.

BUFFERED STANDARD INPUT/OUTPUT

Two sets of routines perform buffered I/O operation. The first implicitly references the terminal that represents the standard input and output files. The other explicitly references a stated file. Both sets have routines that perform single character I/O and formatted I/O.

Single character I/O

The character functions get a character from the standard input and write a character to the standard output. These routines are **getchar** and **putchar**. Their form is simply:

getchar( ) returns the character from standard input (keyboard) or **EOF** (end of file). Depending on the system, it may echo the character to the screen. Note that the returned value of **EOF** may be negative, so assign the returned value to an **int**, not a **char**.

putchar(c) writes the character **c** onto the terminal screen)
int c;

For example:

```
while ((chr=getchar( ))!=EOF)
    {
    putchar(toupper(chr));
    }
```

takes input from the keyboard and puts it onto the screen in upper case.

putchar and **getchar** normally do not concern themselves with any meaning of the characters. Any character may be output. Many video terminals support some form of attribute control, such as cursor positioning. A cursor positioning routine for a typical terminal might look like:

```
#define ESCAPE 27
#define OFFSET 32
cursor(row,column)
/* positions the cursor */
int row;     /* row */
int column; /* column */
    {
    putchar(ESCAPE);
    putchar('=');
    putchar(row+OFFSET);
    putchar(column+OFFSET);
    return;
    }
```

Formatted standard output

The **printf** function acts like a print statement. It is passed a format control string and values to output. The control string gives both the size and interpretation of the values to output and any other characters to output. A special character, **%**, precedes characters that specify the format for the output values. For example, **%d** informs **printf** that an integer value is being passed to it and to convert it to characters and print it. **%f** stands for a floating value, **%s** for a string address and **%c** for a character. The syntax for **printf** is:

printf(*control string,values. . . .*);

where *control string* is a pointer to a string that contains format control and *values* are the values to be printed. Their type should match with the type specified in the format control. The control string is usually written as a string constant though a pointer variable or array name is also valid. For example, if:

```
int i=5;
static char str[5]="ABCD";
```

```
float f=5.2;
char c='z';
```

then

     printf("I=%d Str=%s F=%f C=%c",i,str,f,c);

prints on the terminal:

     I=5 Str=ABCD F=5.2 C=z

If another **printf** follows this one, its first character will be just to the right of the **z**. Note that for **%s** output, the address of the string, which is the name of the character array, is passed to **printf**.

     printf determines the number of values to output from the control string. If fewer values are passed in the parameter list, it will output garbage for those format specifiers.

     Widths can be incorporated in the control string by prefacing the control character with a number. For example, given the declarations above, then

     printf("I=%3d Str=%7s F=%5.1f C=%c\n",i,str,f,c);

yields:

Character

```
0         1         2         3
1234567890123456789012345 67890
I=  3 Str=    ABCD F=  5.2  C=z
```

This is approximately equivalent to the statements in other languages given in Exhibit 8.1. Note that the '**\n**' escape character will cause the next **printf** output to start in the first column of the next line.

     One difference between C and the other languages is the meaning of the field width. In other languages, it states a maximum width. If a number does not fit into it, the value is either truncated on the left side or special characters are printed to show this. In C, the width is the minimum field width. Numbers that take more room will simply use it.

     A print statement does not automatically put a carriage return/line feed at the end of a line. Non-printing characters, including line control, can be output to the terminal using the escape ('****') conventions. For example:

     printf("\nOne line\nTwo line\n");

prints on the terminal:

     One line
     Two line

The next character to be output will be below the **T**.

Full format control using the **printf** function is specified in Appendix D.

Formatted standard input

     Inputting from the standard input is done in a similar manner to **printf**. The routine **scanf** provides formatted input. Its calling sequence is:

     scanf(*control string,variable addresses. . .*);

control string is the format control string

variable addresses are the addresses into which to put the values

The control string may contain both the format for the values to be input and characters that must be present on the input. The format control characters are the same as **printf**. **%d** converts the input characters to an integer. **%f** converts them to a **float** value. **%s** is used for string input, and **%c** is used for single character input. A full discussion of **scanf** formatting is in Appendix D.

The other arguments that are passed to **scanf** are the addresses where the input values are to be put. For example, if:

```
int i;
float f;
char str[5];
char c;
```

and the keyboard input is:

7 ERA 33.2Q

Exhibit 8.1 PRINTF IN OTHER LANGUAGES

BASIC

```
10 PRINT "I=",I," STR=",ST$," F=",F," C=",C$                (unformatted print)
```

MBASIC

```
10 PRINT USING "I=### STR=& F=###.# C=&"; I,ST$,F,C$        (formatted print)
```

FORTRAN

```
       WRITE(6,900) I,STR,F,C
900 FORMAT (3HI=,I3,5H STR=,A7,3H F=,F5.1,3H C=,A1)
```

PASCAL

```
WRITE('I=',I:3,' STR=',STR:7,' F=',F:5:1, 'C=',C:1);
```

PL/I

```
PUT EDIT ('I=', I,' STR=',STR,' F=',F,' C=',C)
     (A,F(3),A,A(7),A,F(5,1),A,A(1));
```

COBOL

```
01 LINE-OUT
       02      FILLER PICTURE XXX VALUE 'I= '.
       02      I       PICTURE 999.
       02      FILLER PICTURE XXXXX VALUE ' STR='.
       02      STR PICTURE XXXXXXX.
       02      FILLER PICTURE XXX VALUE ' F='.
       02      F       PICTURE 999.9.
       02      FILLER PICTURE XXX VALUE ' C='.
       02      C       PICTURE X.

WRITE PRINT-LINE FROM LINE-OUT.
```

then

        scanf("%d%s% f%c",&i,str,&f,&c);

yields:

Variable	Value
i	7
str	ERA
f	33.2
c	Q

Any leading white-space (e.g., blanks, tabs, newline characters) is ignored on the input. For each input value, the characters are read until a white-space character is found or, in the case of numeric values, until a character that could not be part of the value (e.g., for integers '0' to '9' '+' and '−' are valid characters, but only if they come in the proper order). Note that commas are not needed between input numbers and in fact will cause an error. For a string input, the array needs to be large enough to contain the maximum expected input string.

Widths can be incorporated in the format control. These widths are the maximum number of characters that will be scanned if white-space is not found. For example, if the statement reads:

        scanf("%3d%4s%5f%c",&i,str,&f,&c);

and the keyboard input was:

        Character
    0   1
    1234 5 6 7890123456
    116ERAT   3. 2F

then the resulting input would be:

Variable	Value
i	116
str	"ERAT"
f	3.2
c	'F'

In order for **scanf** to work properly, the address of the variable must be passed to it. Thus the address operator (**&**) is included on all variables but **str**. **str** is the name of an array, thus the address of it. Like **printf**, **scanf** determines the number of values to input from the control string. If fewer addresses are present on the parameter list, the program will probably bomb because **scanf** will be attempting to put a value at a garbage address. **scanf** returns the number of values input. If this is less than the number in the control string, then some error on input occurred. If the end of file was reached, then **EOF** will be returned.

The equivalent of **scanf** in other languages is given in Exhibit 8.2.

scanf is not necessarily the best choice for input due to its inability to recover nicely from input errors. Like some other languages, it is useful to input all values as character strings and then use one's own or compiler-supplied conversion routines to change to the required type.

Exhibit 8.2 SCANF IN OTHER LANGUAGES

BASIC

```
10 INPUT I%, STR$, F, C$
```

FORTRAN

```
      READ(5,9000) I, STR, F, C
9000 FORMAT(I3, A4, F5, A1)
```

PASCAL

```
READLN(I : 3, STR : 4, F : 5 : 1, C : 1);
```

PL/I

```
GET EDIT (I, STR, F, C) (I(3), A(4), F(5), A(1));
```

COBOL

```
01 READ-LINE
        05 I     PICTURE 999.
        05 STR   PICTURE XXXX.
        05 F     PICTURE 9999V9.
        05 C     PICTURE X.
        . . .
        READ READ-LINE FROM INPUT-FILE
```

BUFFERED FILE I/O

Files other than the standard input and output must be explicitly opened and referenced. The routines **fopen( )** and **fclose( )** are used to open and close buffered files. Buffered files are referred to by a *file pointer*. This is a system-dependent pointer that is defined in a compiler's **studio.h** file to be a typedef **FILE**. **fopen( )** returns a pointer to a structure of this type. This **file pointer** is used by the other routines to determine which file is to be accessed. **fopen** has the form:

```
FILE *fopen(namefile,mode)
char *namefile;
char *mode;
```

namefile is a character string of the name of the file

mode is a character string that is one of the following:

"**w**" for writing (the previous contents of the file, if any, is cleared)

"**a**" for appending (writes go on end of file)

"**r**" for reading

For example:

```
FILE *filepnt,*fopen( );
    . . .
```

```
filepnt = fopen("NAME","w");
```

opens a file named "NAME" for writing. If any file on the disk is called "NAME", it is cleared out.

Some operating systems make distinctions between text files and binary files. Text files may contain a particular character that signifies the end-of-file, whereas binary files have a count of bytes that determines the end-of-file. The type of file needs to be specified on many systems. The form for doing this varies from compiler to compiler. Some use extensions of the mode string, with the default being a text file. For example:

Mode	Meaning
"rb"	read binary
"wb"	write binary
"rwb"	read and write binary

Single character file I/O

After a file is opened, it may be read from or written to using routines that correspond to those for the terminal. The single character input and output routines corresponding to **getchar** and **putchar** are:

```
getc(filepnt)        returns the next character from the file pointed to by filepnt
FILE *filepnt;

putc(c,filepnt)      puts the character c onto the file pointed to by filepnt
int c;
FILE *filepnt;
```

Formatted file I/O

fprintf and **fscanf** may be used to perform formatted input/output on files that have been opened. The form is:

```
fprintf(filepnt,control string, values. . . .);
```

    filepnt is the file pointer that was returned by **fopen**

    control string is a string containing format control (as in **printf**)

    values are the values (as in **printf**)

```
fscanf(filepnt,control string,variable addresses. . .);
```

    filepnt is the file pointer which was returned by **fopen**

    control string is the format control string (as in **scanf**)

    variable addresses are the addresses into which to put the values (as in **scanf**).

For example, given:

```
char str[ ] = "ABCDE";
FILE *filpnt,*fopen( );
    . . .
filpnt = fopen("SOMEFILE","w");
```

then

    fprintf(filpnt,"%s",str);

puts the string "**ABCDE**" onto the file "**SOMEFILE**".

File closing and deleting

  fclose closes an opened file. Its form is:

    fclose(filepnt)
    FILE *filepnt;

      filepnt is the file pointer returned by **fopen**.

  fclose makes sure that the buffers are flushed to the disk if the file was opened for writing. The compiler usually includes routines that close any opened files if the program terminates normally.

  The function **unlink** removes the named file from the system.

    unlink(name)
    char *name;

      name is the name of the file.

    unlink("TEST");

deletes the file named "**TEST**" (if any) from the disk (or makes it unavailable to the user, depending on the operating system).

UNBUFFERED FILE I/O

  Unbuffered I/O routines directly access devices. These routines do not use a file pointer. Instead they use a *file descriptor*, which is an integer number. By convention, file descriptors of values 0, 1, and 2 are assigned to **stdin**, **stdout**, and **stderr**, respectively.

  These routines are usually called by the buffered routines. A program that uses both buffered calls and unbuffered calls for the same file will have erroneous input or output.

  The function **open** opens an unbuffered file. The syntax is:

    open(name,mode)
    char *name;
    int mode;

      name is the character string of the file name

      mode is the access mode:
        0 for read
        1 for write
        2 for read and write

  open only opens files that exist. To create a file that does not exist, the function **creat( )** is provided. Its syntax is:

```
creat(name)
char *name;
```

> **name** is the character string of the name.

Both of these routines return a file descriptor. The file descriptor is an integer used to reference the file for reading and writing. The functions for those operations are:

```
read(fildes,buffer,count)
int fildes;
char *buffer;
int count;
```

> **fildes** is the file descriptor.
> **buffer** is an address at which to put the bytes read.
> **count** is the byte count to read

```
write(fildes,buffer,count)
int fildes;
char *buffer;
int count;
```

> **fildes** is the file descriptor.
> **buffer** iş the starting address to get the bytes to write.
> **count** is the byte count to write.

The function **close** closes the file referenced.

```
close(fildes)
int fildes;
```

> **fildes** is the file descriptor.

EXAMPLE PROGRAMS

The following example is a file copying program. It copies the file named ''INPUT'' to a file named ''OUTPUT''. In order to simplify it, no checks for error returns have been included.

```
FILECOPY—BUFFERED
#include "studio.h"
main( )
/* Copies INPUT to OUTPUT */
    {
    int c;
    FILE *file1,*file2,*fopen( );
    /* open both files */
    file1 = fopen("INPUT","r");
    file2 = fopen("OUTPUT","w");
    /* loop on each character read */
    while ((c = fgetc(file1))! = EOF)
```

```
            {
            fputc(c,file2);
            }
/* close files */
fclose(file1);
fclose(file2);
exit(0);
}
```

The program could use unbuffered I/O. The following code uses a 128 byte buffer. This might be increased if the disk files had larger physical sectors to increase the speed of the program.

FILE COPY—UNBUFFERED

```
#define SIZE 128
main( )
/* copies INPUT to OUTPUT */
    {
    int fd1,fd2,count;
    char buffer[SIZE];
    /* open files */
    fd1 = open("INPUT",0);
    fd2 = creat("OUTPUT",0);
    /* loop on reads */
    while ((count = read(fd1,buffer,SIZE))>0)
        {
        write(fd2,buffer,count);
        }
    /* close files */
    close(fd1);
    close(fd2);
    exit(0);
    }
```

PIPES AND FILTERS

"Pipes and Filters" is a standard UNIX operating system feature. This feature is being implemented on many microprocessor systems, such as MS-DOS and CP/M (with shell programs). It allows the standard I/O of programs to be redirected on the command line that calls up the execution of the program. For example, suppose a program had been written that converts the typed input into upper case. This program **TOUP** might be written as:

TOUP

```
#include "stdio.h"
main( )
/* outputs input in upper case */
    {
    int chr;
    while ((chr = getchar( ))! = EOF)
```

```
        {
        putchar(toupper(chr));
        }
    }
```

The output of this program would normally be the terminal because **stdout** is directed there by default.

Suppose another program had been written that counts the number of times "THE" appears in the input. This program is called COUNT and might be coded as:

```
COUNT
#include "stdio.h"
main( )
/* counts number of "THE" in input */
    {
    int chr;
    int state=0;
    int count=0;
    while ((chr=getchar( ))!=EOF)
        {
        switch (chr)
            {
            case 'T':
                    state=1;
                    break;
            case 'H':
                    if (state==1) state=2;
                    else state=0;
                    break;
            case 'E':
                    if (state==2) count ++;
                    state=0;
                    break;
            default:
                    state=0;
                    break;
            }
        }
    printf("\nnumber of THE's is : %d", count);
    exit(0);
    }
```

This program will normally take its input (via **getchar**) from the keyboard. If the operating system supports pipes and filters, then the redirection operator | sends the output of one program to the input of another. So

TOUP | COUNT

sends the output from **TOUP** to the input of **COUNT**. The redirection operators > and < are used to redirect the input or output from or to a disk file. The operator >> appends output to an existing disk file.

Diagram 8.1 PIPES AND FILTERS

TOUP | COUNT

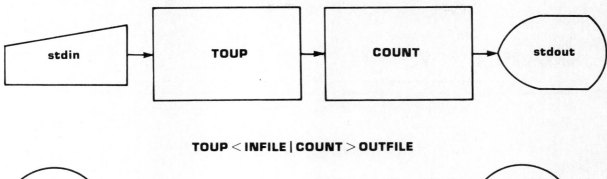

TOUP < INFILE | COUNT > OUTFILE

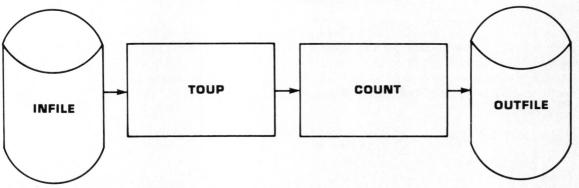

TOUP <INFILE | COUNT >OUTFILE

gets the input for **TOUP** from the file named **INFILE** and passes the output to the input of **COUNT**. The output of **COUNT** is placed on a file named **OUTFILE**. Diagram 8.1 shows this pictorially.

If a program is written with any expectation that it will be used as a filter, error messages should be written to **stderr** rather than to **stdout**. This ensures that the messages appear on the terminal and that they do not get mixed into the output file or get piped to another program.

9

Style

C is like fire. It is powerful, but if it is handled carelessly, one can get burned. Up to now, only the features of C have been covered. This chapter describes how to use the features in a way to assure code readability (maintainability), portability, compactness, and speed. These topics are related in various ways. A portable program is usually readable, but may not be the fastest or the most compact. A fast routine may not be readable or portable. Decisions in these areas require tradeoffs.

READABILITY

C allows the programmer to make a program almost completely unreadable. The examples in this book have followed a similar style to many other program languages. With C, one doesn't have to follow any particular style, but the one described here may make for shorter debugging times, especially when switching from language to language.

Names

Variable names and function names should be lower case. Names that are **#defined** should be uppercase.

Do not reuse variable names within the scope of a routine. That is, although C allows the following declarations, avoid their use.

```
int i;                  external
funct(k,l)
int k,l;                parameters
    {
    . . .
        {
        int i;          local variable within block
        . . .
```

One way to keep external variables straight is to suffix all external variable names with a unique character, such as 'x' or 'z'.

Parentheses

An expression such as **i+ + +2** is perfectly valid. By precedence rules, it is equivalent to **(i+ +)+2**. However, for human readability, it is desirable to include the parentheses. Seeing three **+**'s in a row is sometimes confusing to the eye.

Use parentheses freely. This will ensure that what you meant is what you will get (except for side effects). For example, **(c=a= ='\0')** will be interpreted as **(c=(a= ='\0'))** since **= =** has higher precedence than **=** . So use **((c=a)= ='\0')** if that is what is desired. A common idiom in C is **((chr=getchar( ))!=EOF)**, for which the parentheses are required as in the previous example.

Some of the precedence rules are not self evident. The rules suggest that all bitwise operators be parenthesized. As an example, one might shift an integer three bits to the right instead of dividing it by 8. If **i** had a value of 10, then:

Expression	Value	Notes
5 + i/8	6	
5 + i>>3	1	**+** has higher precedence so this is equivalent to **(5+10)>>3**
5+(i>>3)	6	

Page formatting

There are several ways one can handle indentation and the placement of braces. Usually the code indentation goes over one tab stop when a left brace ({) is encountered and returns one tab stop when a right brace (}) is encountered. Use braces after all constructs like **while**, **do**, **for**, and **switch**.

Indentation can follow one of several conventions. These include:

```
major statement
    {
    minor statements
    }
```

or

```
major statement {
    minor statements
    }
```

or

```
major statement {
    minor statements
    }
```

For example:

Style	Note
while (a>0)	used in this book

```
while (a>0)
    {
    a− −;
    x+ +;
    }
```

Style	Note

while (a>0) {
      a − − ;
      x + + ;
 }
	used by Kernighan and Ritchie

while (a>0){
      a − − ;
      x + + ;
      }
	a combination of above

Pick one style and stick with it.

Externals

Global variable definitions should be put into a header file. Compilers following the Kernighan & Ritchie standard require that they only be defined in one source file, and referenced using **extern** in the other source files. Other compilers allow definitions in each source file. Multiple definitions will be linked together.

If externals are specifically used only in one source file, make them **static**. This keeps them from becoming global externals.

Functions

Keep functions simple. Use clear coding rather than concise coding. Keep track of what modules might be improved with the use of all of C's power. After the program is debugged, the modules can be rewritten. Each function should have a single purpose. This makes them easier to maintain and to rewrite, if required.

Expressions

Keep expressions simple. Use intermediate variables to aid this. Try to keep them looking more like regular procedural language statements. If it takes more than five seconds to figure out what an expression means, it's too complicated.

Use the auto increment and decrement operators and the *op* = freely to save code.

if

Start with using only conditional expressions in **if** tests. For example, use **if (i! = 0)** instead of **if (i)**. These can always be changed later. Besides, the meaning of **0** may change as the program develops. It is better to write it as:

```
#define END 0
    . . .
if (i! = END)
```

If the statement that follows the **if** is simple, keep it on the same line.

Use the **switch** instead of multiple **if** tests if the value of a variable is being compared to several integer constants.

while/for/do-while

The **while, for** and **do-while** constructs do not require a set of braces around the body.

```
while (i = = 5);
```

is a perfectly legal statement. It will loop forever, unless the value of **i** is changed by some external program (such as an interrupt routine). This semicolon might slip in sometimes when one really does not want it there. Since it is somewhat unobtrusive, it is possible to have a program that looks nice, but does not work. One suggestion is to always use braces ({ and }) in the body of loops. Keep the body indented, even if the loop contains only a null statement. The above would then be written as:

```
while (i = = 5)
    {
    ;
    }
```

Likewise:

```
while (x<5)
    x + +;
```

would be written as:

```
while (x<5)
    {
    x + +;
    }
```

With the braces, the meaning is clearer, and if new statements are added to the loop (for debug purposes or whatever), the braces are already there.

goto

goto's should be avoided if possible. C provides numerous structured constructs to eliminate the need for most **goto**s. The **break** and **continue** help in this regard. The main use of a **goto** is to break out of several nested loops.

Programmers who wish to follow ''structured programming'' entirely should never use the **goto**. Others may choose to use a few well-controlled **goto**s to avoid multiple testing of conditions or to exit deeply nested **if** statements.

PORTABILITY

Although C is a portable language, programs can be coded in a manner that prevents them from easily being transferred from machine to machine.

Avoid using anything that makes an assumption about the order in which the bytes of a multi-byte value (such as an integer) are stored in memory. For example, on some computers, the first byte of a two-byte integer has the least significant bits and the second byte has the most significant bits. On other machines, this order is reversed. Treating integers as character strings and vice versa should therefore be avoided. See Diagram 9.1 for an example of what not to do.

Diagram 9.1 EXAMPLE OF MIXING POINTERS

```
int m[5] = {5,7,31,18,22};
char *b;
b = m;
```

Variable	Address	Value
m[0]	630	5
m[1]	632	7
m[2]	634	31
m[3]	636	18
m[4]	638	22
b	800	630

Expression	Value
b	630
*b	contents of 630 (1 byte)
b + 3	633
*(b + 3)	contents of 633 (1 byte)

The contents of 630 may be either the lower or upper byte of **m[0]**, depending on the machine. (See Appendix H on numbers). [1]

Use **typedef**s for variables whose type may need to change from machine to machine for such reasons as the differing size of integers.

The sign extension on **char** values varies from machine to machine. For maximum portability, assume that a character value has a maximum of 127. Do not try to use the high-order bit of characters as a bit flag. Some machines (such as the IBM-PC) use this for extended character sets. The UNIX compiler has an **unsigned char** that treats the variable as an unsigned integer. (See Appendix H for explanation of sign bits).

The actual character used for a newline ('\n') differs among operating systems. Many use the linefeed (ASCII value 10) character, but some use the carriage return (ASCII value 13) character. A few translate the newline character into a carriage return and line feed.

External names are usually significant to seven or eight characters, depending on the compiler and linker. Some linkers do not differentiate between upper and lower case names on externals, so keep all external names unique without regard to case distinctions.

Numeric or alphabetic constants, especially machine dependent ones, should not appear within the body of a program. They should all be defined with **#define** statements, preferably in an **#include** file.

ERRORS

Errors in a program can occur during the compilation phase, (i.e., when the C compiler is attempting to translate a routine) or while the program is executing. Even a program that compiles and executes may not produce the correct results. Those may either be caused by incorrect program design or by mistakes made in writing the C program.

Compiler errors

Look at the first detected error and correct it. A missing brace ({) or similar mistake can cause tens to hundreds of errors to appear as the compiler loses its place in the code.

Execution errors

There are few, if any, checks for execution errors performed by the C language, as compared to other languages. That is, conditions such as reading past the end of a file or a subscript exceeding the size of an array do not cause an error message to appear. Numeric errors such as dividing by 0 or overflowing the value of an integer do not cause C errors, but on some machines may cause an error action to occur.

Writing errors

Because C is a fairly free-form language compared to other languages, many writing mistakes that might be caught by compilers in other languages are not trapped by the C compiler. These mistakes include writing statements that appear perfectly valid, but whose results are not what was intended.

Operators

Watch out for the assignment operator (=) in **if** conditions.

if (x = 5) . . . does something entirely different than **if (x = = 5)** . . . The first expression assigns the value 5 to **x** and has a value that is always true. The second expression is true only if **x** is equal to 5.

Bit operators do something entirely different than logical operators, though they look similar.

Expression	Value
7 && 5	1 (true)
7 & 5	5 bit operator (111 ''and'' 101)
7 || 5	1 (true)
7 | 5	7 bit operator (111 ''or'' 101)

Functions

There is no type checking between the actual and formal parameters of a function. On some systems, a program named **lint** can be used to check the source code for type mismatches and other possible problems of this type. Watch out for passing values to functions that expect pointers. If the function **funct( )** expects a pointer to a simple variable, then **funct(a)** will give entirely different results than **funct(&a)** and may even crash the program. Not passing pointers to **scanf** is a typical program crashing error.

Unless a function is declared as returning a type other than **int**, then C assumes that it returns an **int**. If the function has been defined to return a **float**, then garbage will be returned.

One way to check that functions are sent the proper types of values is to put **printf** calls at the beginning of each function. These calls can be removed after the program is debugged. A **printf** call can be placed just before the **return** statement to check the value computed by the function.

The name of a function by itself is an address. Watch for using a declared function name without the parentheses. For example:

float f( );	declares **f** to be function returning a float.
j = f( );	assigns result of **f** to **j**
j = f;	assigns address of **f** to **j**

Order evaluation

There are no rules for the order of evaluation in an expression. This means that side effects of function calls, assignment operators (=), and postfix and prefix auto increment and decrement operators (+ + and − −) may produce erroneous results. Since evaluation cannot be counted on to take place in a predetermined order, if the order is important, use a temporary variable. For example:

```
int a = 1;            /* global */
. . .
int b;
if (func1( ) + a) b = a;
. . .
func1 ( )
    {
    a = 0;
    return 0;
    }
```

b may be either 0 or 1 after the **if** statement. It will be 0 if **func1** was called first and evaluated. It will be 1 if the value of **a** was evaluated first. If **func1** is definitely to be called first, then use:

```
int a = 1;
. . .
int t;
. . .
t = func1( );
if (t + a) b = a;
. . .
```

Similarly, in function calls, the order of evaluation of the parameters is not guaranteed to be one way or the other. For example, with **func3(func1( ),a);**, func3 may be passed either 0 and 1, or 0 and 0.

Characters and strings

''A'' is not the same as 'A'. The former is a string of characters. It can be used anywhere a character pointer is used. It is a constant that takes up two character locations (one for the terminating null). The latter is a single character. For example:

```
func("A");
```

func will be passed a pointer to the character string **"A"**.

```
func('A');
```

func will be passed the integer value corresponding to **'A'**.

Pointers

Pointers can have integer values added or subtracted. These values are not literally integers, but represent multiples of the size of the data type pointed at. Do not confuse these operations with the regular addition and subtraction of integers.

Diagram 9.2 POINTER USAGE TO AVOID

Do not attempt this, unless absolutely necessary:

char *b = "XYZ";
*b = 'A';

Variable	Address	Value at address	After the second statement address has the value
constant	300	'X'	'A'
constant	301	'Y'	'Y'
constant	302	'Z'	'Z'
constant	303	'\0'	'\0'
b	800	300	300

A "constant" has been destroyed.[2]

C allows for the testing of equality of pointers. Pointers are often compared to 0 (**NULL**, the invalid pointer). Do not attempt to compare pointers for greater than or less than; they may have the integer equivalents of a negative value.

Watch out for omitting the indirection operator (*) when a pointer is used. Given:

> **int *q,r;**
> **q = &r;**

then

> **q = 5;**

does something entirely different than

> ***q = 5;**

In the first expression, the value of **q** is changed. In the second, the value of **r**, which **q** points at, is changed.

Do not use a pointer until it has a valid address. Watch out for overwriting constants, as in Diagram 9.2.

Do not return the address of an **auto** class variable from a function. The storage location will be used for other **auto** class variables. See Appendix F for a discussion on storage usage.

Arrays

Do not take the address of name of an array, since the name itself is an address. Array subscripts start at 0 rather than at 1, as in many other languages.

DOCUMENTATION SUGGESTIONS

Programs should have enough comments so that not only other persons can understand what is going on, but also so the programmer can remember why it was written the way it was six months after he or she coded it. In addition, certain documentation standards can help increase code maintainability.

Header files

Use one **#include** file for all external (global) variables and function declarations that return non-integers and structure tag-type definitions. Include a description of each program global variable in this file. Use another **#include** file for all **#define**s. If the operating system allows extensions on file names, use an extension of ''h''.

Function files

Include a one-line description of each function immediately after the function name.

Explicitly declare all the formal parameters.

Include a description of the parameters in comments just after the declarations.

Include a description of the return value. Either always set the return value to something or never set it (leave it garbage). Follow the precepts of good program structure and use only one **return** in a function. Although a **goto** to that **return** may be necessary, a single point of return simplifies testing.

Put all the documentation of a function in comments in the code. If it is in a separate place, it may never change when the code changes or the person looking for it may not be able to find it.

Use white space liberally.

Avoid long expressions. If an expression is longer than a line, try to break it up with some temporary variables. Avoid also putting too many expressions in **while** and **for** tests to eliminate bodies of loops.

According to the informal laws of computing, 90% of the time is spent in 10% of the code. Write clean code, and keep an eye out for real time wasters (such as excessive parameter passing). Don't make the code ''tricky'' in the beginning just to save execution time. If the modules have been properly broken up, only a few will need to be rewritten, perhaps in assembly language, to give the proper speed. The reason for higher level languages is to make the code readable and maintainable. Do not forsake clarity of purpose for speed.

Try to keep each function to one or two printed pages. This allows it to be read without flipping pages and makes it short enough to be quickly recoded if speed requirements dictate. Use explicit returns in functions and a single call to **exit( )** in the main program (or a second one in a fatal error handling routine).

COMPACTNESS

Due to the restricted memory space available on microcomputers, it is important to write a compact program. Although a good C compiler produces relatively tight code, there are a few hints on how to write the more compact code.

The first is in the use of variables. Although **static** integers take up a few bytes of memory, on many eighty-eight machines a reference to a **static** integer takes up less memory than a reference to an **auto** integer. If the routine is going to be re-entrant or recursive, then **static** integers should not be used. Other than these cases, making integers **static** saves memory. On many sixteen-bit machines, the reverse is true.

If the integer variables need to be **auto**, then making them **register** will save space on many machines.

Character arrays, unless they need to be initialized, usually require less space if they are **auto**. The **auto** attribute allows the space to be reused by other routines. If a temporary space for keyboard input is required, then a global array for this use may save some memory. In general, using pointers to sequentially access arrays is faster and more compact than using indexes.

Minimize the number of formal arguments in functions. Each argument takes up space in both putting it on the stack and clearing it off. Pass a pointer to a structure instead. This works especially well with constant type data (such as writing a string to a specific location on the screen). For example, the function:

```
wrstr(line,col,string)
int line,col;
char *string;
```

would be called by:

```
wrstr(5,8,"output");
```

Instead, create a global structure:

```
struct strs {
int line;
int col;
char *string;
    }
```

and make the function:

```
wrstr(str)
struct strs *str;
```

which may be called by:

```
static struct strs s={5,8,"output");
. . .
wrstr(&s);
```

Furthermore, if the arguments do not get above the value 127, then the structure could be defined as

```
struct strs {
    char line;
    char col;
    char *string;
    }
```

Using global variables in a program (e.g., static globals), reduces the size of the generated code. Instead of passing parameters back and forth within routines in a source file, try to organize the code to reference local globals (**static** externals). This cuts down on the overhead of passing parameters back and forth. Although this violates the structured program design, the tradeoff is advantageous if the global is kept within one code file.

Computing the value of an expression that is used more than once will save code. Though some compilers attempt to optimize code by recognizing these recomputations, other do not. For example:

```
for (i=0;i<n;i++)
    {
    a[i]=k+j;
    }
```

should be replaced by:

```
m = k + j;
for (i = 0;i<n;i + +)
    {
    a[i] = m;
    }
```

The *op* = operator ensures that the computation of an expression will take place only once. For example, if a[i + 2] = a[i + 2] + 5; was replaced by a[i + 2] + = 5;, then the value of i + 2 would be computed only once.

Setting a simple variable to the value of the member of a structure whose address is passed to a function will save code if that member is used frequently. For example,

```
struct stype {
    int j;
    int k;
    };
. . .
func(s)
struct stype *s;
    {
    register int i;
    i = s − >j;
    . . .
```

Using **i** instead of **s** − >**j** will save code in **func** if the value of **s** − >**j** is used more than a couple of times. If the value of **s** − >**j** is to change, then an assignment **s** − >**j** = **i**; can be placed just before the **return** of the function.

SOFTWARE DESIGN

Top-down design of a program starts with an overall layout of the flow. This normally includes an initialization phase, a process phase, and a termination phase. Each of these phases is broken down into subphases, which may be broken down further into subsubphases and so forth.

After writing several programs, the programmer may note that certain operations keep reappearing, such as getting a numeric string from the terminal and signaling an error if the value exceeds certain limits. A programmer can then begin to make up specific routines for operations that are repeatedly used. These routines are called ''software tools.'' C is an ideal language for creating these tools because of its speed and relative compactness.

After creating and debugging (or purchasing) such tools, the top-down design should be influenced by them. Although it might be slightly more awkward to incorporate them in the design, the program creation process will be faster and more reliable.

Footnotes

1. Some compilers may not allow the expression **b** = **m** but will allow **b** = (*char)**m**. This cast forces the assignment of a character type pointer. 2. Some compilers that do not follow the Kernighan and Ritchie standard store all constants having the same value in the same location. The above code would change the ''constant'' everywhere in the program.

Conclusions

The C language is almost like a game of ''GO'' or ''OTHELLO''. Its syntax and grammar is simple. It may take a short time to learn C, but a long time to truly appreciate its complexity.

APPENDIX A   SAMPLE PROGRAMS

These sample programs show a variety of applications in the C language. They include a pair of compression/decompression programs, a sort/search program, a random file update program, and a linked list program.

COMPRESS/DECOMPRESS

In order to save disk space when storing files or communication time when transmitting them to other computers, a process called compression can be used. Compression eliminates having to store or send strings that are repetitions of the same character. Whenever a compression program finds such a string, it substitutes a special character (a compression character), a character count, and one copy of the duplicated character. For example:

Let **&** be the compression character.

Given the input string:

ABCDDDDDEF

then the compressed output string is:

ABC&5DEF

An offset of '0' has been added to the character count to make it appear on the terminal. Depending on the communication channel, no offset or an offset of ' ' (ASCII value 32) may be required. Flowchart A.1 gives the arrangement of a compression program.

```
COMPRESS
#include "stdio.h"

#define MINCOMP 3 /* minimum number of chars to compress */
#define COMPCHAR '&' /* compression character */
#define OFFSET '0' /* offset to use for repetition count */
#define MAXCOMP 126-OFFSET /* maximum number of chars to compress */
main ( )
/* compresses the character string on stdin and puts it onto stdio */
    {
    int oldc=0;
    int repcnt=0;
    int c;

    /* the test for \n is for terminal input */
    while ( ((c=getchar( )) != EOF) && (c!='\n') )
        {
        if (c= =oldc)
            {
            /* if duplicate character, increment repetition counter */
```

129

Flowchart A.1 COMPRESSION

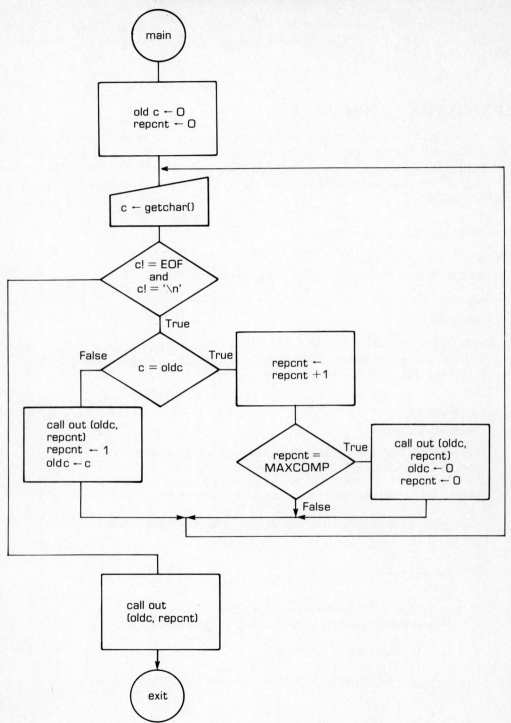

Flowchart A.1 (continued)

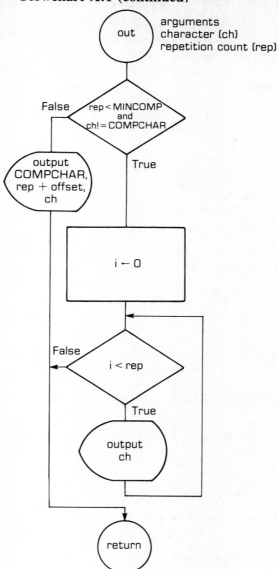

```
                              repcnt + +;
                              if (repcnt = = MAXCOMP)
                              {
                              out(oldc,repcnt);
                              oldc = 0;
                              repcnt = 0;
                              }
                       }
                else
                       {
                       /* output the previous character */
                       out(oldc,repcnt);
                       repcnt = 1;
                       oldc = c;
                       }
                }
         /* output the last character */
         out(oldc,repcnt);
         exit(0);
         }
 out(ch,rep)
 int ch;
 int rep;
 /* outputs appropriate string for a character ch that has appeared rep times */

         {
         int i;
         if (rep < MINCOMP && ch !=COMPCHAR)

                {
                /* less than the minimum to compress and not equal to the compression
                   character */
                for (i = 0;i<rep;i + +)
                       {
                       putchar(ch);
                       }
                }
         else
                       {
                       /* compression string */
                       putchar(COMPCHAR);
                       putchar (rep + OFFSET);
                       putchar (ch);
                       }
                }
```

The corresponding program decompresses the string. Wherever it sees the compression character, it outputs the appropriate number of characters. Flowchart A.2 shows one possible decompression routine.

DECOMPRESS

```
#include "stdio.h"
#define COMPCHAR '&' /* these #defines might be defined in a #include file that would be
    in both programs */
#define OFFSET '0'
main( )
/* decompresses input on stdin and puts it on stdout */
    {
    int state=0;
    int c,i,repcnt;
    /* the test for '\n' is for terminal input */
    while ( ((c=getchar( ))!=EOF) && (c!='\n'))
        {
        switch(state)
            {
        case 0:
            /* if compression character, don't output it*/
            if (c!=COMPCHAR) putchar(c);
            else state=1;
            break;
        case 1:
            /* previous char was compression char current char is repetition count */
            repcnt=c-OFFSET;
            state=2;
            break;
        case 2:
            /* this is the character to output repcnt time */
            for (i=0;i<repcnt;i++)
                {
                putchar(c);
                }
            state=0;
            break;
            }
        }
    exit(0);
    }
```

CHECKBOOK PROGRAM

This program inputs checks and deposits from the terminal, stores them on a file and outputs a new balance. A file "**TRANSFIL**" is created that contains records of all the checks and desposits entered. It might be read by another program and printed out or used for further processing of some kind. Flowchart A.3 gives the outline.

Flowchart A.2 DECOMPRESSION

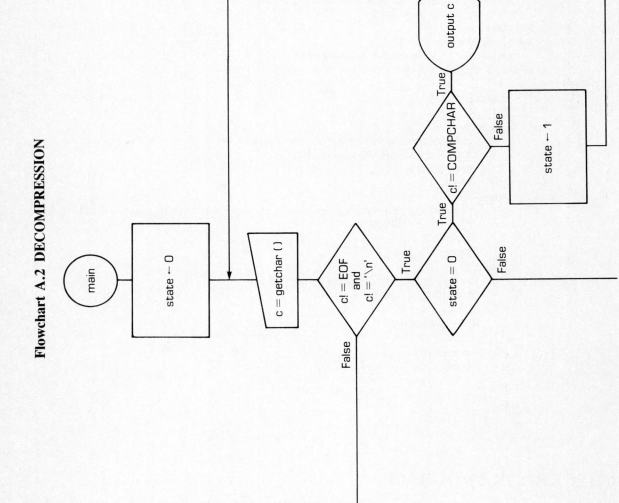

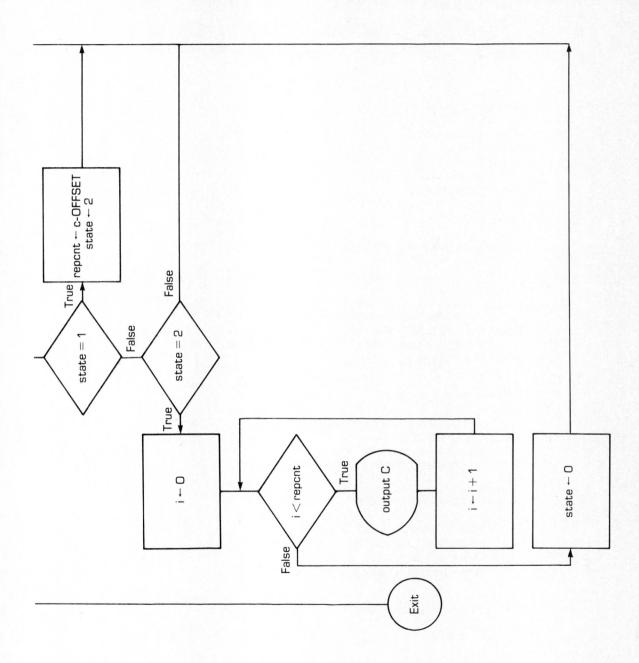

CHECKBOOK

```
#include "stdio.h"
main( )
/* computes the current balance of a checking account. saves checks and deposits on
    transfil */
{
FILE *transfil,*fopen( );
float check = 0.0;
float deposit = 0.0;
float oldbal = 0.0;
float newbal,amount;
char type = 0;
int again = 1;
printf("\nEnter old balance ");
scanf("%f",&oldbal);
transfil = fopen("TRANSFIL","w");
if (transfil = = NULL)
    {
    printf("\nunable to open transaction file");
    exit(1)
    }
while (again)
    {
    /* if previous type not newline or space, give prompt */
    if ((type! = '\n')&&(type! = ' '))
            printf("\nEnter type (C)heck,(D)eposit (E)nd: ")
    scanf("%c",&type);
    amount = 0.0;

    if (toupper(type) = = 'D')
            {
            printf("\nEnter deposit amount ");
            scanf("%8f",&amount);
            deposit + = amount;
            fprintf(transfil,"Deposit %12.2f\n",amount);
            }

    else if (toupper(type) = = 'C')
            {
            printf("\nEnter check amount ");
            scanf("%8f",&amount);
            check + = amount;
            fprintf(transfil,"Check %12.2f\n",amount);
            }

    else if (toupper(type) = = 'E')
            {
            again = 0;
            }
```

Flowchart A.3 CHECKBOOK PROGRAM

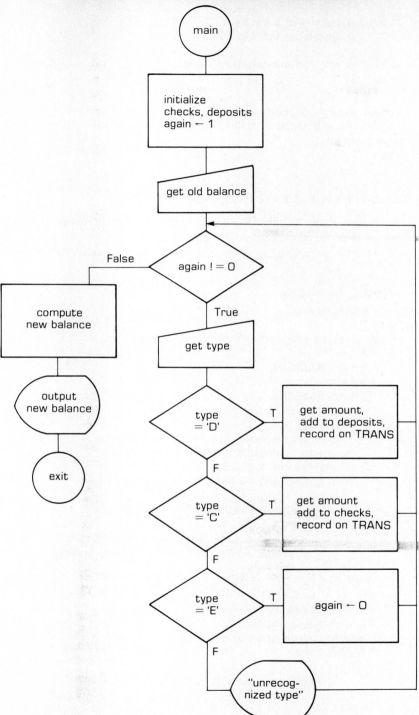

```
        else if (type! = '\n' && type! = ' ')
                /* ignore spaces and newlines */
                {
                printf("\nUnrecognized type");
                }

        }
newbal = oldbal + deposit − check;
printf("\nNew balance is %12.2f",newbal);
fclose(transfil);
exit(0);
}
```

SORT AND BINARY SEARCH ROUTINES

This program demonstrates a bubble sort routine and a binary search routine. The program first sorts an array that is input, outputs the sorted array, and then asks for a number to search for. To simplify the program, an input of 0 is considered to be the end of the input. The flowchart for the sort and search routines is A.4.

```
SORT AND SEARCH
#define MAXNUM 100
main( )
/* inputs, sorts, and searchs a string of integers */
        {
        int arr[MAXNUM];
        int size = 0;
        int ret, num, fnd;
        while (1)
                {
                /* input numbers till 0 or an error in scanf */
                printf("\nInput a number, 0 to start sort ");
                ret = scanf("%d",&num);
                if ( (num! = 0) && (ret = = 1) )
                    {
                    if (size<MAXNUM) arr[size + +] = num;
                    else
                        {
                        printf("\nNo more room, starting sorting");
                        break;
                        }
                    }
                else break;
                } /* end while */
        printf("\nsize of array is %d",size);
        if (size = = 0)
                {
                printf("\nno input");
                }
        else
                {
                printf("\nUnsorted array");
```

```
                prtarr(arr,size);
                sort(arr,size);
                printf("\nSorted array");
                prtarr(arr,size);
                /* ask for input numbers */
                while (1)
                    {
                    printf("\nNumber to look for (0 to end) ");
                    ret=scanf("%d",&num);
                    if ((ret==1)&&(num!=0))
                        {
                        fnd=binsrch(arr,size,num);
                        if (fnd>=0)
                            {
                            printf("\n%d is in array",num);
                            printf("\nindex is %d",fnd);
                            }
                        else printf("\n%d is not in array",num);
                        }
                    else break;
                    } /* end while */
                } /* end else */
end:    exit(0);
                }
prtarr(arr,nitem)
/* prints nitems in integer array arr */
int arr[];
int nitem;
                {
                register int i;
                for (i=0;i<nitem;i++)
                    {
                    if (i%10==0) printf("\n");
                    printf(" %d ",arr[i]);
                    }
                return;
                }
sort(arr,nitem)
/* sorts nitem in integer array arr */
int arr[];
int nitem;
                {
                register int i,notdone,temp;
                if (nitem<=1) goto end;
                do
                    {
                    notdone=0;
                    i=0;
                    do
                        {
                        if (arr[i]>arr[i+1])
                            {
```

Flowchart A.4 PROGRAM TO BUBBLE SORT AND BINARY SEARCH

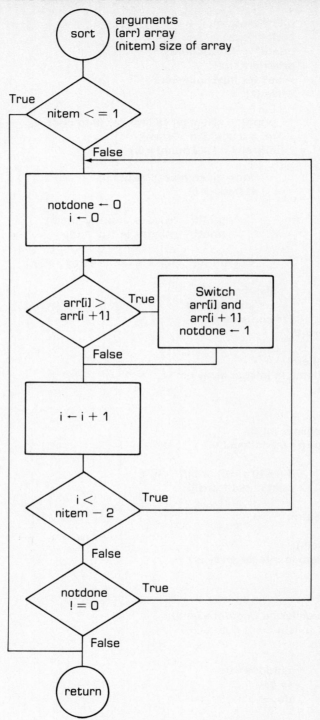

arguments
(arr) array
(nitem) size of array

140

Flowchart A.4 (continued)

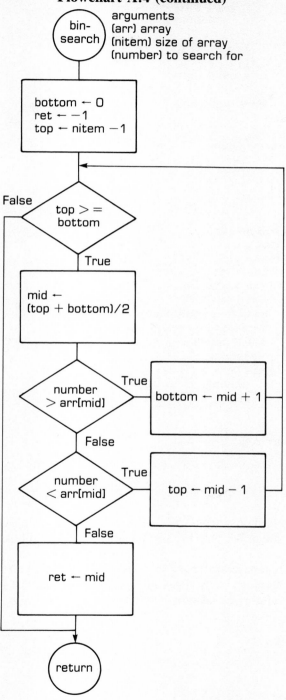

bin-search

arguments
(arr) array
(nitem) size of array
(number) to search for

bottom ← 0
ret ← −1
top ← nitem −1

top >= bottom

False / True

mid ← (top + bottom)/2

number > arr[mid]

True → bottom ← mid + 1

False

number < arr[mid]

True → top ← mid − 1

False

ret ← mid

return

```
                                temp = arr[i];
                                arr[i] = arr[i + 1];
                                arr[i + 1] = temp;
                                notdone = 1;
                                }
                        i + + ;
                        }
                while (i<(nitem − 2));
                }
                while (notdone);
end:        return;
        }
binsrch(arr,nitem,number)
int arr[ ];
int nitem;
int number;
        {
        int mid;
        int bottom = 0;
        int top;
        int ret = − 1;
        top = nitem − 1;
        while (top> = bottom)
                {
                mid = (top + bottom)/2;
                if (number>arr[mid]) bottom = mid + 1;
                else if (number<arr[mid]) top = mid − 1;
                /* found it */
                else {
                    ret = mid;
                    break;
                    }
                }
        return ret;
        }
```

LINKED LIST

A linked list is composed of structures that point to each other. Diagram A.1 shows an example of a singly linked list. This program adds links to a list and prints out the list. Flowchart A.5 gives a way to add a node to a linked list.

A system dependent routine **lalloc( )** must be written. It can call **malloc** to allocate memory, but it must ensure that the pointer it returns correctly aligns all the members of **link**. To avoid system dependencies, in this version **lalloc** simply returns the address of an element in a static array.

LINK LIST

```
#include "stdio.h"
struct link {
```

Diagram A.1 LINKED LIST EXAMPLE

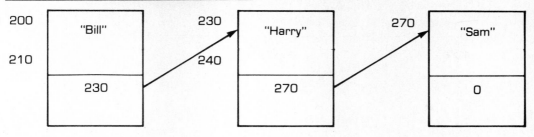

```
            char string[10];
            struct link *next;
            };
        main( )
        /* This program adds links and prints a list of links */
            {
            int chr=0;
            char str[81];
            while (1)
                {
                if ( chr!=' ' && chr != '\n')
                    {
                    printf("\nType A to add a link");
                    printf("\nType P to print links");
                    printf("\nType E to end\n");
                    }
                chr=getchar( );
                if (chr==EOF) break;
                chr=toupper(chr);
                if (chr=='E') break;
                if (chr=='A')
                    {
                    printf("\nType string to add: ");
                    scanf("%80s",str);
                    addlink(str);
                    }
                else if (chr=='P')
                    {
                    printf("\nLinks are:");
                    printf("\nCount is: %d \n",prtlink( ));
                    }
                }
            exit(0);
            }
        struct link root={NULL,NULL};
        struct link *start=&root;
        int init=0;
```

Flowchart A.5 LINKED LIST

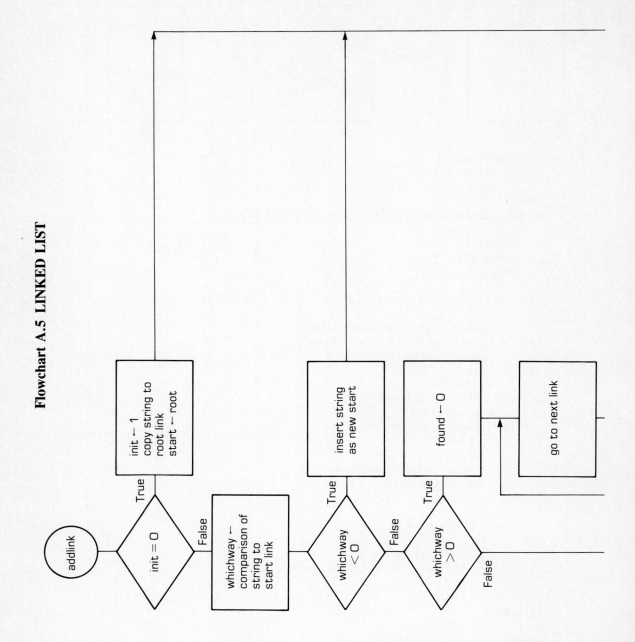

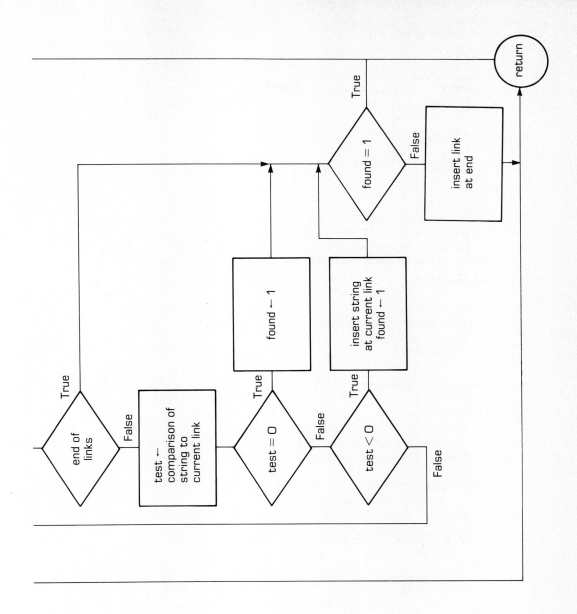

```
addlink(instr)
/* adds a link to singly linked list */
char *instr;
    {
    int found,whichway,test;
    struct link *new,*prev,*lalloc( ),*current;
    if (init= =0)
        {
        /* this is the first link */
        init=1;
        strcpy(start->string,instr);
        }
    else
        {
        whichway=strcmp(instr,start->string);
        /* whichway is 0 if strings match */
        /* is <0 if instr comes before start */
        /* is >0 if instr comes after start */

        if (whichway<0)
            {
            new=lalloc( );
            strcpy(new->string,instr);
            new->next=start;
            start=new;
            }

        else if (whichway>0)
            {
            current=start;
            found=0;
            /* search list for where to put string */
            while (current->next!=NULL)
                {
                prev=current;
                current=prev->next;
                test=strcmp(instr,current->string);

                /* test= 0 duplicate */
                if (test= =0)
                    {
                    found=1;
                    break;
                    }

                /* test < 0 string comes before current */
                else if (test<0)
                    {
                    found=1;
                    new=lalloc( );
```

```
                        strcpy(new − >string,instr);
                        prev − >next = new;
                        new − >next = current;
                        break;
                        }

                /* test > 0 keep going */
                } /* end while */

            if (!found)
            /* ran past last link without setting up new link */
                {
                new = lalloc( );
                current − >next = new;
                new − >next = NULL;
                strcpy(new − >string,instr);
                }

            } /* end else on whichway */
        } /* end else on init */
    return 0;
    }
prtlink( )
/* prints the links in order */
/* returns number of links */
    {
    struct link *current;
    int count;
    count = 0;
    if (init = = 0)
        {
        printf("\n no links ");
        }
    else
        {
        current = start;
        do
            {
            printf("\nlink %d is %s", count, current − >string);
            current = current − >next;
            count + + ;
            }
        while (current! = NULL);
        }
    return count;
    }
struct link *lalloc( )
        {
        static struct link m[100];
        static int count = 0;
```

```
/*
This is machine dependent. If the computer requires certain alignment on pointers,
it must be altered to reflect that
*/
if (count = = 100)
    {
    printf("\nout of memory");
    exit(1);
    }
return &m[count + +];
}
```

RANDOM FILE MAINTENANCE

This is a file maintenance program for random records. It keeps a file of records that have a name, city, and state for each record. The program allows one to add records or print records. Flowchart A.6 gives the flow.

```
FILE UPDATE
#include "stdio.h"

#define SIZENAME 20
#define SIZECITY 20
#define SIZESTATE 10
#define ESCAPE 27 /* Used as character to end input */
#define NAMEFILE "TESTFILE" /* Name of file for records */

/* this is the record layout */
struct srecord {
    char name[SIZENAME];    /* Name */
    char city[SIZECITY];    /* City */
    char state[SIZESTATE]; /* State */
    };
#define SIZEREC sizeof(struct srecord)
        /* Size of record in bytes */
struct srecord record;
struct sflddes {
    char *field;    /* Points to field of record */
    char *label;    /* Label for that field */
    char size;    /* Size in bytes of field */
    } flddes[ ] =
            {
            {record.name,"Name",SIZENAME},
            {record.city,"City",SIZECITY},
            {record.state,"State",SIZESTATE}
            };
#define NUMFLD sizeof(flddes)/sizeof(struct sflddes)
        /* Number of fields in record */
```

```
main( )
/* Adds records and prints a random file */
    {
    static union {
        struct srecord u;
        int reccnt;
        } firstrec; /* This is the first record with count of number of records */
    FILE *filnam,*fopen( );

    int c=0;
    firstrec.reccnt=0;
    /* Check to see if file exists */
    if ((filnam=fopen(NAMEFILE,"r"))==NULL)
            {
            printf("\nNew file");
            /* write first record */
            filnam=fopen(NAMEFILE,"w");
            wrrec(filnam,&firstrec,0,SIZEREC);
            fclose(filnam);
            }
    else
            {
            /* get number of records */
            rdrec(filnam,&firstrec,0,SIZEREC);
            printf("\nOld file record count %d",firstrec.reccnt);
            fclose(filnam);
            }
    while (1)
        {
        printf("\nType A to Add records \n");
        printf("Type P to Print records \n");
        printf("Type E to End \n");
        while (getfld(&c,1)<=0)
            {
            ;
            }
        c=toupper(c);
        switch(c)
            {
            case 'A':
                /* Open to append records */
                filnam=fopen(NAMEFILE,"a");
                while (getinp(firstrec.reccnt+1)>=0)
                    {
                    wrrec(filnam,&record,++firstrec.reccnt,SIZEREC);
                    }
                fclose(filnam);
                break;
```

```
case 'P':
        /* These closes and opens make the routine more portable. The
           file could actually be opened and closed only once if read/
           write access was allowed
        */
        filnam = fopen(NAMEFILE,"r");
        prtall(filnam,firstrec.reccnt,SIZEREC);
        fclose(filnam);
        break;
case 'E':
case EOF:
        filnam = fopen(NAMEFILE,"a");
```

Flowchart A.6 RANDOM FILE

Flowchart A.6 (continued)

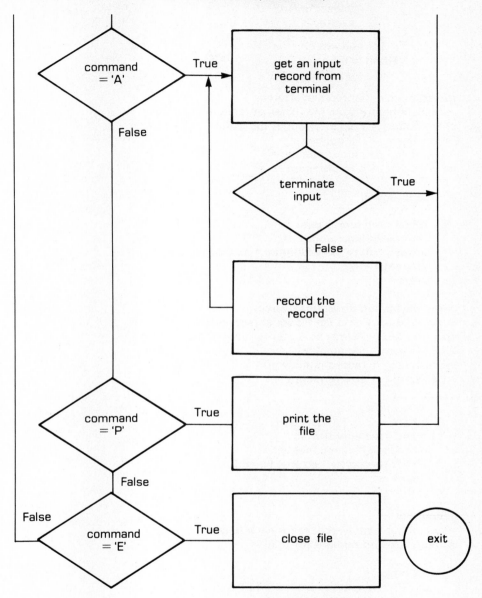

```
            wrrec(filnam,&firstrec,0,SIZEREC);
            fclose(filnam);
            exit(0);

      } /* end switch */
   } /* end while */
}

rdrec(filnam,buffer,recnum,sizerec)
/* reads a record from file filnam at recnum position */
char *buffer; /* Pointer to buffer for read */
FILE *filnam; /* file pointer */
int recnum;   /* record number */
int sizerec;   /* size of record */
   {
   long offset;
   int ret;
   offset = recnum*sizerec;
   ret = fseek(filnam,offset,0);
   if (ret = = 0) ret = fread(buffer,1,sizerec,filnam);
   else ret = - 1;
   return ret;
   }
wrrec(filnam,buffer,recnum,sizerec)
/* writes record onto file filnam at recnum position */
char *buffer; /* Pointer to buffer to write */
FILE *filnam; /* file pointer */
int recnum;   /* record number */
int sizerec;   /* size of record */
   {
   long offset;
   int ret;
   offset = recnum*sizerec;
   ret = fseek(filnam,offset,0);
   ret = fwrite(buffer,1,sizerec,filnam);
   return ret;
   }

getinp(rec)
/* gets input from keyboard for each field */
int rec; /* record number for print */
   {
   int ret,i;
   printf("\nInput record %d Hit ESC to end\n", rec);
   clear(&record,SIZEREC,0);
   for (i=0;i<NUMFLD;i+ +)
      {
      printf("\n%s: ",flddes[i].label);
      ret = getfld(flddes[i].field,flddes[i].size);
```

```
        if (ret<0) break;
        }
    return ret;
    }

getfld(buffer,n)
/* reads a field, returns −1 if ESC pressed else number of characters read */
char *buffer; /* Pointer to field */
int n;          /* size of field */
    {
    int c,ret;
    clear (buffer,n,0);
    ret=0;
    while ( (n−−) && (c=getchar( ))!='\n' && c!=ESCAPE )
        {
        ret++;
        *buffer++=c;
        }
    if (c==ESCAPE) ret=−1;
    /* don't use rest of input till end of line */
    if (c!='\n')
        {
        while ( (c=getchar( )) !='\n' )
            {
            if (c==ESCAPE) ret=−1;
            }
        }
    return ret;
    }

prtall(filnam,reccnt,sizerec)
/* prints the records in filnam */
FILE *filnam; /* file pointer */
int reccnt;    /* number of records */
int sizerec;   /* size of record */
    {
    int i,j;
    printf("\nRecord count is %d\n",reccnt);
    for (i=1;i<=reccnt;i++)
        {
        rdrec(filnam,&record,i,sizerec);
        printf("\nRecord %d is:",i);
        for (j=0;j<NUMFLD;j++)
            {
            printf("\n%s: ",flddes[j].label);
            prtfld(flddes[j].field,flddes[j].size);
            }
        }
    printf("\n");
```

```
        return sizerec;
        }

    prtfld(field,size)
    /* Prints a single field */
    char *field; /* Pointer to field */
    int size;    /* Size of field */
        {
        while (size - -)
            {
            putchar(*field + +);
            }
        return;
        }
```

SCREEN MENU DISPLAY

This program displays a main menu screen and two submenus. It is a demonstration as to how one might construct menus with C, as well as keep machine dependent output functions modular and hidden from other routines. Flowchart A.7 gives the flow of this program.

```
DISPLAY
#include "stdio.h"
#define ESCAPE 27
#define OFFSET 32
struct sline {
    int row;
    int col;
    char *string;
    };
static struct sline screen1[ ]={
    {5,5,"Do you want to know about "},
    {7,10,"1. What this program does"},
    {9,10,"2. How this program works"},
    {11,10,"3. Exit this program"},
    {13,10."ENTER # AND RETURN"}
    };
int size1 = sizeof(screen1)/sizeof(struct sline);
static struct sline screen2[ ]={
    {5,5,"It demonstrates menu selections"},
    {7,5,"Enter C to go back"},
    };
int size2 = sizeof(screen2)/sizeof(struct sline);
static struct sline screen3[ ]={
    {5,5,"Enter C to go to next screen"},
    };
int size3 = sizeof(screen3)/sizeof(struct sline);
static struct sline screen4[ ]={
```

```
            {5,5,"This program is written in C"},
            {7,5,"Enter C to go to main menu"},
            };
int size4 = sizeof(screen4)/sizeof(struct sline);
main( )
    {
    int c;
    int d = 0;
    while (1)
        {
        /* display main screen */
        if (d = = 0) dspscr(screen1,size1);
        cursor(20,20);
        c = getchar( );
        switch(c)
            {
            case '1':
                dspscr(screen2,size2);
                keyin('C');
                d = 0;
                break;
            case '2':
                dspscr(screen3,size3);
                keyin('C');
                dspscr(screen4,size4);
                keyin('C');
                d = 0;
                break;
            case '3':
                exit(0);
                break;
            default:
                d = 1;
                break;
            }     /* end switch */
        }     /* end while */
    }     /* end main */

dspscr(screen,numline)
/* display a screen */
struct sline screen[ ]; /* array of lines */
int numline;            /* number in array */
    {
    register int i;

    clrsc( );
    for (i = 0;i<numline;i + +)
        {
        dspline(&screen[i]);
```

Flowchart A.7 SCREEN MENUS

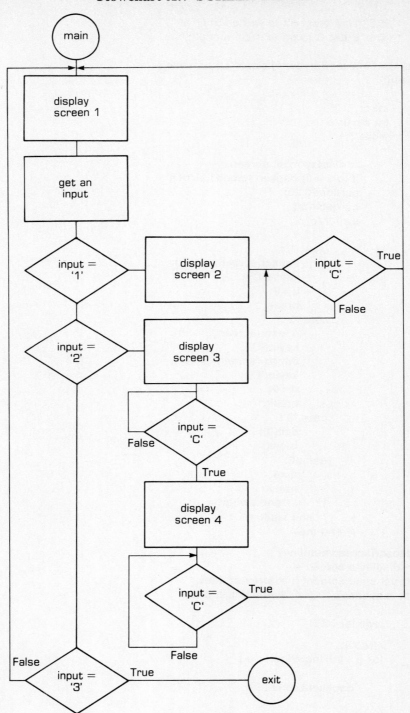

```
            }
      return 0;
      }
dspline(line)
/* prints line on terminal screen */
struct sline *line; /* line to print */
      {
      cursor(line->row,line->col);
      strout(line->string);
      return 0;
      }

cursor(row,col)
/* positions cursor at row,col
   no check made on validity of row and col
   This is terminal dependent          */
int row; /* row */
int col;  /* column */
      {
      putchar(ESCAPE);
      putchar('=');
      putchar(OFFSET+row);
      putchar(OFFSET+col);
      return;
      }

strout(string)
/* outputs a string to terminal, not including null char */
/* no check is made for error on output */
char *string; /* string to output */
      {
      while (*string)
            {
            putchar(*string++);
            }
      return 0;
      }

clrsc( )
/* clears the screen */
/* this is terminal dependent */
      {
      putchar(ESCAPE);
      putchar('v');
      putchar(ESCAPE);
      putchar('T');
      putchar(ESCAPE);
```

```
            putchar('0');
            putchar('@');
            putchar(ESCAPE);
            putchar('9');
            putchar('P');
            return 0;
            }
    keyin(chr)
    /* waits till chr is pressed */
    int chr; /* character to wait for */
        {
        while (1)
            {
            cursor(20,20);
            if (chr = =toupper(getchar( ))) break;
            }
        return chr;
        }
```

FUN WITH C ROUTINE

A program dedicated to the Beatles:

```
    main( )
        {
    while (9)
        {
        9;
        }
    }
```

The usual program for demonstrating a C compiler is:

```
    main( )
        {
        printf("\nhello world\n");
        }
```

An alternative is:

```
    main( )
        {
        char *malloc( ) ,*b;
        printf("\ngoodbye world");
        b=malloc(1);
```

```
while (1)
    {
    *(b++)=0;
    }
}
```

APPENDIX B   SUMMARY OF C

	Page
Variables	
char	7
int	7
float	7
long	8
short	7
unsigned	8
double	7
typedef	95
Constants	
character	9
string	9
integer	9
octal	9
hexidecimal	9
float	9
Storage classes	
auto	11
static	11
extern/external	50
register	12
Expressions	
general	
operators	12

unary
++ --	15
~	14
&	14
!	13
sizeof	61
*	12

binary
* - / + %	14
& |	14
&& ||	13
>> <<	14
== <= >= > < !=	12
=	14
,	16
op =	14
.	11

tertiary
?:	15

precedence	18

Statements

simple ;	18
compound { }	20

Control-flow

if, **else**	22
while	27
do-while	29
for	30
switch, **case**, **default**	37
break	34
continue	34
goto, *label*	40

Compound variables

Arrays [ ]	55
Structures **struct** .	59
Unions **union**	65

Pointer variables

*	73
&	73

APPENDIX C   C EQUIVALENTS

BASIC	**C Equivalent**	**Page**
CALL assembly language routine	function	5
CLOSE	**fclose( )**	109
DATA—to set things to be READ (for initializing)	initializers	190
DEF—a function	function	43
DIM	**[ ]**	56
END	**exit( )**	4
FOR,TO,STEP/NEXT	**for**	33
GET	**getchar( )**	110
GOSUB	function	46
GOTO	**goto**	28
IF,THEN/ELSE	**if**	23
INPUT	**scanf( )**	109
LET(=)	**=**	17

BASIC	C Equivalent	Page
ON X GOTO	**switch**	39
ON X GOSUB	**switch**	39
OPEN	**fopen( )**	111
PEEK	pointers	74
POKE	pointers	74
PRINT	**printf( )**	107
PUT	**putchar( )**	105
READ (DATA)	initializers	190
REM	/* */	21
RETURN	**return**	190
STOP	**exit( )**	102
WRITE	**printf( )**	107
# (double)	**double**	8
$ (character)	**char**	8
% (integer)	**int**	8
Operators:		
+ − * /	+ − * /	17
< > <= >= <>=	> < <= >= != == =	17
MOD	%	17
AND OR NOT	& | !	17

FORTRAN	C Equivalent	Page
CALL subroutine	function( )	46
COMMON	externals	51
COMPLEX	not supported	
CONTINUE	see DO or GOTO	
DATA—initialization	initializers	
DECODE	**sscanf( )**	109
DIMENSION	**[ ]**	56
DO	**for**	20
ELSE	**else**	24
ELSE IF	**else if**	24
ENTRY	not supported	
EQUIVALENCE	**union**	67
FORMAT	format string	107
FUNCTION	function	43
GO TO	**goto**	41
IF	**if**	23
IMPLICIT	not supported	
INCLUDE	**#include**	94

FORTRAN	C Equivalent	Page
INTEGER	**int**	8
LOGICAL	not necessary	
PAUSE	**printf( ) & getchar( )**	107
PRINT	**printf( )**	107
PROGRAM	**main( )**	49
READ	**scanf( )**	109
REAL	**float**	8
RETURN	**return**	42
REWIND	**fseek( )**	173
STOP	**exit( )**	102
SUBROUTINE	function	46
WRITE	**printf( )**	107
Statement function	function	46
Operators:		
EQ NE XOR OR AND NOT	== != && || !	17
GT LT GE LE NE EQ	> < >= <= != ==	17
+ − * /	+ − * /	17

PASCAL	C Equivalent	Page
ARRAY	[ ]	56
BEGIN	{	20
BOOLEAN	not needed	
CASE	**switch**	39
CHAR	**char**	8
CONST	**#define**	92
DO	see corresponding keyword	
DOWNTO	**for**	33
ELSE	**else**	24
END	see corresponding keyword	
FILE	file pointer	82
FOR	**for**	33
FUNCTION	function	43
GOTO	**goto**	28
IF	**if**	23
IN	enumeration	102
INTEGER	**int**	8
LABEL	:	17
MOD	%	17
NIL	**NULL**	75
NOT	!	17

PASCAL	C Equivalent	Page
OF	arrays of structures	56
OR	||	17
PACKED	not supported	
PROCEDURE	function	46
PROGRAM	**main( )**	49
READ	**scanf( )**	109
REAL	**float**	8
RECORD	**struct**	74
REPEAT	**do-while**	31
SET	enumeration	102
TEXT	**char[ ]**	8
TO	**for**	33
TYPE	**typedef**	60
UNTIL	**do-while**	31
VAR	declaration	56
WHILE	**while**	29
WITH	not supported	
WRITE	**printf( )**	107
:=	**=**	17
< <= = <> >= >	**< <= == != >= >**	17
+ − * /	**+ − * /**	17
AND,OR,NOT	**&&, || ,!**	17
MOD	**%**	17
DIV	/ (with integers)	17

PL/I*	C Equivalent	Page
ADDR	**&**	177
ALLOCATE	**malloc**	74
BASED	pointers	74
BEGIN	**{**	20
CALL	function	46
CHARACTER	**char**	8
CLOSE	**fclose( )**	5
DECLARE	declarations	51
DECLARE 1. . .	structures	60
DEFINED	**union**	67
DO	**{**	20
DO variable = . . .	**for**	33
DO WHILE	**while**	29

*Note that not all PL/I keywords are listed.

PL/I	C Equivalent	Page
DO UNTIL	**do-while**	31
END	**}**	20
EXTERNAL	externals	51
FIXED BINARY	**int**	8
FLOAT	**float**	8
GET EDIT, GET LIST	**scanf( )**	109
GO TO	**goto**	41
IF	**if**	23
INITIAL	initializers	62
OPEN	**fopen( )**	111
POINTER	pointers	74
PROCEDURE	functions	43
PROCEDURE OPTIONS(MAIN)	**main( )**	49
PUT EDIT, PUT LIST	**printf( )**	107
PUT SKIP. . .	**printf(" \n \n. . . .)**	107
RECORD	structures	74
RETURN	**return**	46
SELECT	**switch**	39
STATIC	**static**	62
WHILE	**while**	29
Operators		
+ − * /	**+ − * /**	17
MOD	**%**	17
< > <= >= =	**< > <= >= ==**	17
& |	**& |**	17
	&& ||	17
¬	**!**	17

COBOL*	C Equivalent	Page
ACCEPT	**getchar( ), scanf( )**	107
AT END	**EOF**	105
CALL	function	46
CLOSE	**fclose( )**	5
COMPUTE	**=**	29
DEPENDING ON	**switch**	39
ELSE	**else**	25
END	**exit( )**	102
FILE	file pointer	5
FOR	**for**	33
GOTO	**goto**	41

*Note that not all COBOL Keywords are listed

COBOL*	C Equivalent	Page
IF	**if**	23
INDEXED	**[ ]**	55
INITIAL	initializers	62
OCCURS	**[ ]**	55
OPEN	**fopen( )**	5
READ	**read( )**	5
REDEFINES	**union**	67
REWIND	**fseek( )**	173
SPACE	**' '**	108
PICTURE 999V999	**float**	8
PICTURE 999	**int**	8
PICTURE XXXX	**char [ ]**	8
PICTURE . . .	format control	8
PERFORM . . . VARYING	**for**	20
PERFORM . . . UNTIL	**while**	20
RECORD	**struct**	59
STOP RUN	**exit( )**	5
UNTIL	**while**	29
WRITE	**printf( )**	107
Operators:		
LESS THAN (<)	**<**	17
GREATER THAN (>)	**>**	17
EQUAL TO (=)	**= =**	17
AND OR NOT	**&& || !**	17
+ − * /	**+ − * /**	17

APPENDIX D   INPUT/OUTPUT ROUTINES

A number of standard input and output routines are supplied with most compilers. These routines have slight variations among operating systems based on the types of files that a system supports.

The **#include** file **stdio.h** that is supplied with compilers contains the definition of **EOF**, the end-of-file flag; **NULL**, the invalid pointer; **FILE**, the typedef for file pointers; and the three standard file pointers—**stdin**, **stdout**, and **stderr**.

BUFFERED INPUT/OUTPUT

```
FILE *fopen(name,mode)
char *name;
char *mode;
```

Opens a file named **name** for buffered access according to the **mode**. The three modes that are commonly supported are:

"**r**" for reading only

"**w**" for writing only—this discards any data if the file already exists

"**a**" for appending to the end of an existing file

The return value is a file pointer for the file or **NULL** if the file cannot be opened. The file pointer is used in all other operations with this file. Since files can only be opened for reading or writing, many compilers include additional modes that allow simultaneous reading and writing, such as might be performed on a random access file.

FILE *freopen(name,mode,filepnt)
char *name;
char *mode;
FILE *filepnt;

Attaches a new file to previously opened file pointed at by **filepnt**. The old file is closed. The **name** and **mode** are the same as **fopen**. The return value is also the same. This function is usually used to reassign **stdin**, **stdout**, or **stderr**, because these files are automatically opened when a program is executed.

fread(buffer,itmsize,numitm,filepnt)
char *buffer;
int itmsize;
int numitm;
FILE *filepnt;

This reads **numitm** items of size **itmsize** from the file pointed at by **filepnt** and puts them starting at the address pointed to by **buffer**. The return value is the number of items read. This value may be less than **numitm** if an error or end of file occurred.

fwrite(buffer,itmsize,numitm,filepnt)
char *buffer;
int itmsize;
int numitm;
FILE *filepnt;

This writes **numitm** items of size **itmsize** to the file pointed at by **filepnt** from the address pointed to by **buffer**. The return value is the number of items written. This value may be less than **numitm** if an error occurred.

fclose(filepnt)
FILE *filepnt;

This closes the file pointed to by **filepnt**. It flushes any data in the buffer and closes the file. The return value is **EOF** if there was an error, or 0 otherwise.

getc(filepnt)
FILE *filepnt;

This gets the next character in the file pointed to by **filepnt**. The return value is the character or **EOF** if it is the end of file. Note that **EOF** is usually set to -1 in many systems. To test for this, the returned value should be assigned to an integer variable rather than a character variable. A character variable may not be able to have a value of -1, depending on the computer.

putc(chr,filepnt)
int chr;
FILE *filepnt;

This puts the character **chr** into the file pointed at by **filepnt**. The return value is **EOF** if an error; otherwise, the value of **chr**.

fgetc(filepnt)
FILE *filepnt;

This does the same thing as **getc**. **getc** is usually a macro that is expanded in-line. **fgetc** is commonly the linkable routine. The return value is same as **getc**.

fputc(chr,filepnt)
int chr;
FILE *filepnt;

This does the same thing as **putc**. **putc** is usually a macro that is expanded in-line. **fputc** is commonly the linkable routine. The return value is same as **putc**.

getchar( )

The return value is the next character from the standard input. The value is **EOF** if end-of-file. This is usually a macro call to **getc(stdin)**.

putchar(chr)
int chr;

This puts the **chr** character onto the standard output. This is usually a macro call to **putc(chr,stdout)**. The return value is **chr** or **EOF** if an error occurred.

ungetc(chr,filepnt)
int chr;
FILE *filepnt;

This pushes back the character **chr** back onto the file pointed at by **filepnt**. The character does not have to be the same one as that gotten by the last **getc**. The next

getc for this file will return this character. Only one character of pushback is allowed for each file. The return value is **chr** if the routine is successful, otherwise **EOF**.

char *gets(buffer)
char *buffer;

This reads characters from the **stdin** file until an end-of-line or end-of-file character is received. The characters are stored at the address given by **buffer**. The end-of-line or end-of-file character is not stored, but a terminating null byte is stored at the end. The return value is **buffer** if everything was okay, or it is **NULL** if an error occurred or end-of-file happened before any character was received.

puts(buffer)
char *buffer;

This writes the string pointed at by **buffer** to the standard output file. The string is output until the terminating null is encountered. The null byte is not written, but a newline is output at the end. The return value is **EOF** if any errors are encountered.

fgets(buffer,max,filepnt)
char *buffer;
int max;
FILE *filepnt;

This reads the file pointed at by **filepnt** until a newline or **max**-1 characters have been read. The characters are read into **buffer**. The newline is included in the string. The last character is followed by a null character. The return value is **buffer** if the routine is successful, otherwise it is **EOF** or **NULL** for an error or end-of-file.

fputs(buffer,filepnt)
char *buffer;
FILE *filepnt;

This writes the string pointed at by **buffer** to the file pointed to by **filepnt**. The terminating null byte is not written. The return value is **EOF** if an error ocurred.

FORMATTED INPUT CONVERSIONS

scanf(format, *pointers*...)
char *format;
----- *pointers* (can be any type)

This reads the standard input file according to the **format** and puts the data at the addresses specified by the *pointers*. The return value is the number of items for which valid input was found. If an error or end-of-file occurred, the return value is **EOF**.

fscanf(filepnt,format, *pointers...***)**
FILE *filepnt;
char *format;
---- *pointers* (can be any type)

This reads the file pointed to by **filepnt** according to the **format** and puts the data at the addresses specified by the *pointers*. The return values are like **scanf**.

sscanf(buffer,format, *pointers...***)**
char *buffer;
char *format;
---- *pointers* (can be any type)

The string pointed at by **buffer** is scanned according to the **format** and the data is put at the addresses specified by the *pointers*. The return value is the number of items for which valid input was found. If an error or end-of-string occurs, the return value is **EOF**.

Formatting on input

The format for input is a string of characters. Each item in the string that begins with a % is a format specifier. The format specifier has the form:

$$\%*wlX$$

where * is optional and means that the conversion is to be performed, but the result value is not put anywhere. This is useful for sets of input that are formatted, but for which only a portion of the input is required by a program.

w is a decimal number specifying the maximum field length. It is optional.

l indicates that the matching pointer is to a **long integer** or a **long float** (i.e. **double**). It is optional.

X is one of the following:
  d—decimal integer
  o—octal integer
  x—hexidecimal integer
  h—short integer
  c—single character
  s—character string
  f—floating point number

White space characters in the format are ignored. Non-white space characters, other than the format specifiers, must match the corresponding non-white space characters in the input string. White space characters in the input string are ignored, except for single character input (**%c**), which uses the next character regardless of whether it is a white space character.

Format	Corresponding pointer	Notes
d	integer	
o	integer	input may or may not have leading 0
x	integer	input may or may not have leading 0x
u	integer	unsigned integer
h	short integer	
c	character	skip over white space is not done. Next input character is returned. If next non-white character is wanted, use %1s.
s	character	pointer should be to variable array big enough to hold the string plus null character that is added.
f or **e**	float	input may have optional sign, a optional decimal point, and optional exponent field starting with E or e followed by signed or unsigned integer.
l	long integer	
lx	long integer	hexidecimal input
lo	long integer	octal input
lf or **le**	long float	double precision input

Input for numbers stops at the first nonvalid character if the field length has not been reached.

Note that the arguments to the scan routines must be pointers. A field is a string of non-white space characters. It extends either to the next white space character or until the field width, if any is specified, is completed. White space is blanks, tabs, newlines, and comments.

There are potential problems with **scanf**. If an error occurs in the input string, the scanning stops there. If **scanf** is immediately called again, the scanning will restart there. For example, if:

```
scanf("%d",&intvar)
```

and the input typed in from **stdin** is:

```
ABC
```

then **scanf** will return a 0. If it is called again with the same format, it will continue to return a 0.

FORMATTED OUTPUT

```
printf(format, arguments...)
char *format;
----- arguments (various types)
```

This prints values of *arguments* on **stdout** according to the **format** control string.
The return value is the number of characters written or **EOF** if an error occurred.

```
fprintf(filepnt,format, arguments...)
FILE *filepnt;
charc*format;
----- arguments
```

This prints values of *arguments* on the file pointed to by **filepnt** according to the **format** control string. The return value is the same as **printf**.

sprintf(string,format, *arguments***...)**
char ∗string;
char ∗format;
----- *arguments*

This puts the values of *arguments* into the string pointed at by **string** according to the **format** control string. The return value is the same as **printf**.

Formatting of output

The format specifiers for output are of the type:

$$\%-w.plx$$

− (optional) indicates the field is left justified

w is the minimum field width. More will be used if necessary.

. separates the numbers *w* and *f* if *p* is used

p is the maximum field width for a string or the precision for a floating point number (number of digits after the decimal point)

l indicates the corresponding argument is a long type

x is one of the following:

    d—decimal signed integer
    u—decimal unsigned integer
    x—hexidecimal integer (no leading 0x)
    o—octal integer (no leading 0)
    s—character string
    c—single character
    f—fixed decimal floating point number
    e—exponential floating point number
    g—either **f** or **e**, whichever is shorter

Characters that are not in format specifiers are output directly. If the character following a **%** is not a format specifier, then it is printed.

If the converted item has fewer characters than the minimum field length, then:

    If − was present, left justify (pad on right)

    Otherwise right justify (pad on left)

    If field length *w* began with a 0, then use 0 to pad, otherwise use space (' ').

Format Specifier	Argument	Notes
s	string pointer	printed until null or maximum field width (*w*)

Format Specifier	Argument	Notes
e	float or double	output is of form: $(-)x.xxxxxxE(+/-)xx$ where the precision (p) specifies the number of digits after the decimal point. Default precision is 6.
f	float or double	output is of form: $(-)xxx.xxxxxx$ where the precision (p) specifies the number of digits after the decimal point. Default is 6.
g	float or double	**e** or **f** is used, whichever is shorter.

BUFFERED FILE OPERATIONS

fseek(filepnt,offset,mode)
FILE *file;
long offset;
int   mode;

This positions the file pointed to by **filepnt** to a new position so the next character read from that file is from that position.

> **mode** = 0 position to **offset** bytes from beginning of file
> = 1 position to **offset** bytes from current position
> = 2 position to **offset** bytes relative to end of file

The return value is **EOF** if error occurs. Example of calls are:

Function call	Result
fseek(filepnt,0L,0)	file positioned at beginning (equals a rewind)
fseek(filepnt,0L,2)	file positioned at the end (to append to it)
fseek(filepnt,5L,1)	file positioned 5 bytes past current position.

long ftell(filepnt)
FILE *filepnt;

The return value is the current position in the file referenced by **filepnt** or **EOF** if an error occurred.

rewind(filepnt)
FILE *filepnt;

This rewinds the file referenced by a **filepnt**. (Performs an **fseek(filepnt,0L,0)).**

ferror(filepnt)
FILE *filepnt;

The return value is non-zero if an error occurred while reading or writing the file pointed to by **filepnt**. Otherwise zero.

clearerr(filepnt) or clrerr(filepnt)
FILE *filepnt;

This resets the error indication on the **filepnt** file. Until this function file is called, once an error condition occurs on a file, **EOF** will be the returned value on all functions concerning it.

fileno(filepnt)
FILE *filepnt;

The return value is the file descriptor used by the system input/output routines associated with the file **filepnt**.

fflush(filepnt)
FILE *filepnt;

This forces the internal buffer of the **filepnt** file to be written; that is, it flushes the buffer. The return value is **EOF** if any errors occurred or 0 otherwise.

UNBUFFERED INPUT/OUTPUT

These are system level input/output routines that are usually called by the buffered I/O routines and may be called directly by a program. Using an unbuffered call to access characters in a file opened as a buffered file may result in erroneous data. The files for system level input/output are accessed using a file number or file descriptor, which is just an integer. Usually the compiler reserves file descriptor values 0, 1, and 2 for standard input (**stdin**), standard output (**stdout**), and standard error output (**stderr**). This is a carryover from UNIX operating system conventions.

There are a few problems in porting ASCII files. Some operating systems use line-feed as the end of line delimiter, others use carriage return, and still others use carriage return/line feed. Some compilers provide ways of automatically translating these. One solution may be to use either the carriage return or the line feed and to use a **#define** to state which one is to be used for a particular system.

open(filename,mode)
char *filename;
int mode;

Opens a file with the system name **filename**.

      mode   = 0 opened for read only
                = 1 for write only
                = 2 for reading and writing

The file is positioned to the beginning, if it can be opened.

The return value is the file descriptor if successful, otherwise a negative value. This file descriptor is used in the other operations on this file.

creat(filename,mode)
char *file;
int mode;

This opens a file with the system name **filename** for writing. If the file exists, it is deleted. The **mode** bits are system dependent. The return value is the file descriptor if successful, otherwise a negative value.

unlink(filename)
char *filename;

This removes the **filename** file from the system. The return value is 0 if successful, otherwise a negative number.

read(filedes,buffer,count)
int filedes;
char *buffer;
int count;

This reads **count** bytes from the file referenced by **filedes** to the address starting at **buffer**. The return value is 0 if end-of-file occurred, less than 0 if an error occurred, or the number of bytes read.

write(filedes,buffer,count)
int filedes;
char *buffer;
int count;

This writes **count** number of bytes starting at **buffer** to the file referenced by **filedes**. The return value is less than 0 if an error occurred or the number of bytes written.

long lseek(filedes,offset,mode)
int filedes;
long offset
int mode;

This positions the file referenced by **filedes** to the position specified by **offset** and **mode**.

> **mode** =0 **offset** relative to beginning of file
> =1 **offset** relative to current file position
> =2 **offset** relative to end of file

The return value is less than 0 if an error occurred or the new file position. Examples of calling this function are:

Function call	Result
lseek(filedes,0L,0)	file positioned at beginning (equals a rewind)
lseek(filedes,0L,2)	file positioned at the end—(to append to it)
lseek(filedes,5L,1)	file positioned 5 bytes past current position.

```
close(filedes)
int filedes;
```

This closes the file referenced by **filedes**. This return value is less than 0 if an error occurred or 0 if successful.

```
exit(retcode)
int retcode;
```

This flushes and closes all open files. It returns to the operating system with a return code of **retcode**.

```
_exit(retcode)
int retcode;
```

This terminates the program immediately without closing or flushing files. It returns the value of **retcode** to the operating system.

APPENDIX E   COMMON FUNCTIONS

This is a listing of common functions that are usually supplied with a C compiler. Some of the functions, especially the memory allocation ones, are machine dependent and may be written in either the machine's assembly language or in C. Others may simply be C routines, such as were shown in several examples in this book. **NULL** is usually defined in the **stdio.h** file included with most compilers.

MEMORY ALLOCATION ROUTINES

These routines provide for allocation and deallocation of blocks of memory. (See Appendix F.)

```
char *malloc(size)
int size;
```

This allocates a block of memory of **size** units (usually bytes). The return value is a pointer to the memory or **NULL** if memory was not available.

```
char *calloc(numel,elsize)
int numel,elsize;
```

This allocates a block of memory for **numel*elsize** units. The return value is a pointer to the memory or **NULL** if memory was not available.

> **free(addr)**

This releases a block of memory at address **addr** that was allocated by either **malloc** or **calloc**. Attempting to release a block that was not allocated or using a bad address may cause serious problems.

UTILITY ROUTINES

> **clearmem(addr,count,chr)** (this has many names)
> **char *addr;**
> **int count;**
> **char chr;**

This stores the character **chr** repetitively in **count** bytes of memory starting at address **addr**.

> **movmem(dest,source,count)**   (this also has many names)
> **char *dest;**
> **char *source;**
> **int count;**

This moves **count** bytes of memory from address starting at **source** to address starting at **dest**. The function checks the relative location of source and destination and ensures that the move is done in the proper order if the blocks overlap.

CHARACTER ROUTINES

These may be implemented as macros. Sometimes they use an array which is indexed by the character itself.

isdigit(c)	Return value is 0 if **c** is not a digit (character '0' to '9') ! = 0 if **c** is a digit
isalpha(c)	Return value is ! = 0 if **c** is alphabetic character. = 0 if **c** is not
islower(c)	Return value is ! = 0 if **c** is lower case character. = 0 if **c** is not
isupper(c)	Return value is ! = 0 if **c** is upper case character. = 0 if **c** is not

isspace(c)   Return value is
                   ! = 0 if **c** is white space (blank, tab or newline)
                   = 0 if **c** is not

toupper(c)   Return value is
                   = **c** in upper case if **c** is lower case
                   = **c** unchanged otherwise[1]

tolower(c)   Return value is:
                   = **c** in lower case if **c** is upper case
                   = **c** unchanged otherwise[1]

STRING ROUTINES

strlen(string)
char *string;

The return value is the number of bytes in the **string** not counting the null terminating byte.

char *strcpy(dest,source)
char *dest;
char *source;

This moves the entire string from **source** to the address given by **dest**. The terminating null is moved. The return value is **dest**.

char *strcat(dest,source)
char *dest;
char *source;

This concatenates the **source** string onto the end of the **dest** string. A null terminator is included. The return value is **dest**.

strcmp(string1,string2)
char *string1;
char *string2;

This compares **string1** to **string2** character by character. When the characters do not match or the terminating byte is reached on both strings, the result is returned. The return value is:

  0 **string1** matches **string2**
 <0 **string1** is less than **string2**
 >0 **string1** is greater than **string2**

Footnotes

1. The UNIX version of **toupper** may multilate non-letters and should be preceded by a **islower** test. The same applies to **tolower**.

APPENDIX F   MEMORY USAGE IN C

A C program in memory can be divided into four basic parts. These are the code segment, the data segment, the stack, and the heap. Depending on the compiler, these parts may be further subdivided. The arrangement of these memory sections vary from compiler to compiler. However, a typical compiler uses memory as described below. Diagram F.1 depicts the layout.

CODE AND DATA

The code segment contains the executable machine instructions of the program. It usually is put in the lowest addresses in memory. Some operating systems may reserve the first few hundred addresses (starting at location 0) for scratchpad use. In that case, the code starts above those locations.

The data segment contains the static and external variables. This resides just above the code segment.

STACK AND FUNCTIONS

The stack section is controlled by the stack pointer. This is a compiler or machine variable that points to the highest available memory location. When a value is "put on the stack", the stack pointer is decremented, and the value is stored at the memory location pointed to by the stack pointer. When a value is "popped off the stack," the value is retrieved from the location pointed at and the stack pointer is incremented.

When a function is called, the values of the arguments, if any, are put on the stack one by one. The address to which it should return is then put on the stack, and control is transferred to the first instruction in the function. At the beginning of the function, **auto** variables are allocated by decrementing the stack pointer by a value equal to the number of bytes required for them.

When a function returns, the stack pointer is incremented by the number required for the **auto** variables. Then the return address is popped off and control is transferred back to that address. The calling routine then increments the stack pointer by the number of bytes that were required for the arguments.

A typical passing of parameters is shown in Diagram F.2. Note that a machine register is usually used for the value returned by a function. The C code for this example is from Chapter 4.

Diagram F.1 TYPICAL MEMORY LAYOUT FOR C PROGRAM

Top	Operating System
	Stack
	Heap
	Data Segment
	Code Segment
	Operating System
Bottom	Reserved Area

Diagram F.2 STACK DURING A FUNCTION CALL

BEFORE THE CALL

Stack pointer

892

DURING EXECUTION OF **addone**

Stack pointer

886

Address	Usage
886	**outnum**
888	return address to calling routine
890	5 (value passed as argument)

AFTER THE RETURN:

Stack pointer

892

Machine register (for return value)

6

```
j=addone(5);
. . .
addone(innum)
int innum;
    {
    int outnum;
    outnum=innum+1;
    return outnum;
    }
```

Diagram F.3 demonstrates what occurs in a stack with a function that is called recursively. The code for this example is from Chapter 7. To demonstrate **auto** variable allocation, a temporary variable has been added.

```
factor(3);
. . .
factor(i)
int i;
    {
    int temp;
    if (i==0) temp=1;
    else  temp=i*factor(i-1);
    return temp;
    }
```

Diagram F.3 STACK DURING RECURSIVE FUNCTION CALL

Stack pointer during call to	Address	Usage
factor(0)	1002	**temp**
	1004	return address
	1006	0 (value of parameter)
factor(1)	1008	**temp**
	1010	return address
	1012	1 (value of parameter)
factor(2)	1014	**temp**
	1016	return address
	1018	2 (value of parameter)
factor(3)	1020	**temp**
	1022	return address
	1024	3 (value of parameter)
calling routine	1026	last **auto** variable

DYNAMIC MEMORY ALLOCATION

The ''heap'' is a section of memory that is used for dynamic allocation of storage. This section usually resides just above the data segment and below the section used by the stack. When a program needs a block of storage, it may call a compiler-supplied allocation routine (**calloc** and **malloc** are the usual names). These routines determine whether there is sufficient memory to allocate and what part of memory to allocate. The calling routine is free to do whatever it wishes with the allocated memory. Once it is finished with it, it should return it to the heap for reuse. The routine commonly named **free( )** is called to do this.

The heap is typically used for large arrays that need to be accessed from several different routines and whose sizes may vary for each execution of a program.

APPENDIX G   FLOWCHART SYMBOLS

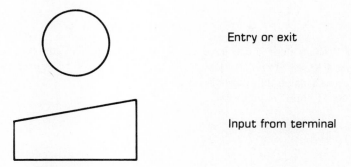

Entry or exit

Input from terminal

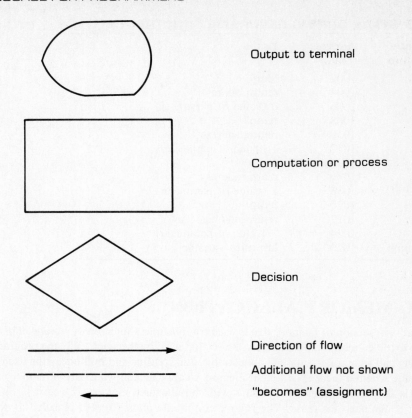

Output to terminal

Computation or process

Decision

Direction of flow

Additional flow not shown

"becomes" (assignment)

APPENDIX H   BITS, BYTES, AND NUMBERS

The following is a brief explanation of terms relating to bits, bytes, and numbers.

BITS

A bit (short for "binary digit") can have the value of 0 or 1. The common operations with bits are NOT, AND, OR, and EXCLUSIVE-OR. The NOT operation inverts the value of a single bit. The other three operations produce a value that depends on two bits.

The value for "NOT bita" is given by:

Bita	Value
0	1
1	0

For example, ''NOT 1'' has a value of 0.
The value for ''bita AND bitb'' is given by:

Bita	Bitb	Value
0	0	0
0	1	0
1	0	0
1	1	1

For example, ''1 AND 0'' has a value of 0.
The value for ''bita OR bitb'' is given by:

Bita	Bitb	Value
0	0	0
0	1	1
1	0	1
1	1	1

For example, ''1 OR 1'' has a value of 1.
The value for ''bita EXCLUSIVE-OR (or XOR) bitb'' is:

Bita	Bitb	Value
0	0	0
1	0	1
0	1	1
1	1	0

For example, ''1 XOR 0'' has the value 1.

A string of bits may be combined with another string of bits using these operators. The value of the result is determined by applying the operation to each bit pair. As an example, the result of ''11010 AND 10111'' is determined by:

Bita	AND	Bitb	Value
1		1	1
1		0	0
0		1	0
1		1	1
0		1	0

so the resulting string is ''10010''.

Binary arithmetic

A string of bits has an arithmetic value. Each bit position has a value that is equal to twice that of the bit position to the right. For example, the arithmetic value of ''01101010'' is determined by:

Bit position	7	6	5	4	3	2	1	0
Value of bit position	128	64	32	16	8	4	2	1
Example bit string	0	1	1	0	1	0	1	0

$$
\begin{array}{r}
64 \\
+32 \\
+\ 8 \\
+\ 2 \\
\hline
106
\end{array}
$$

Arithmetic value of the bit string is

In the typical computer, strings of 8 or 16 bits are used to store numbers. The leftmost bit (called the most significant bit or MSB) may be used to store the sign of a number. Typically the sign is 0 for a positive number and 1 for a negative number. The range of values that an 8-bit string can have is from 0 to 255, if the MSB is not used for a sign (i.e., unsigned), or -128 to $+127$ if the MSB is the sign. For a 16 bit string, the range is 0 to 65,535 for unsigned numbers and $-32,768$ to $+32,767$ for signed numbers.[1]

Sign extension

If a string of 8 bits is expanded to a string of 16 bits, the top 8 bits may either be set to 0 or may depend on the sign bit of the 8 bits. The latter case is called sign extension. If the sign bit of the 8-bit number is a 1, then the leftmost 8 bits of the 16-bit number are each set to 1. For example:

8-Bit number	16-Bit number	
	Without Sign Extension	*With Sign Extension*
01101110	0000000001101110	0000000001101110
10010000	0000000010010000	1111111110010000

Shifts

A bit string can be shifted left or right. If the string is shifted left, the rightmost bit (least significant bit or LSB) is set to 0. If the string is shifted right, the MSB may be set to either 0 (termed a logical shift) or it may keep its starting value (termed an arithmetic shift). These two types of shifts differ if the MSB or sign bit is a 1. For example, for a shift of a single bit place:

8-Bit number	Logical shift		Arithmetic shift
	Left	*Right*	*Right*
01001001	10010010	00100100	00100100
10011000	00110000	01001100	11001100

Bit string representation

Instead of using 1's and 0's to represent bit strings, two other common representations are used—octal and hexidecimal. In octal notation, a digit can have a value of 0 through 7. Each digit represents three binary digits. In hexidecimal notation, the digits can have a value of 0 through 15. The values above 9 are represented by "A" through "F". Each digit represents four binary digits.[2] If the leftmost bits of a binary string are 0, these are usually not included in the octal or hexadecimal form. For example:

Binary string	Octal string	Hexidecimal string
001	1	1
1000	10	8
10001000	210	88

Binary string	Octal string	Hexidecimal string
1010	12	A
1111	17	F
11111111	377	FF

BYTE

A set of 8 bits is commonly called a byte. The value of the byte may refer to a character. Which character it refers to is only a convention. Two common conventions are ASCII (American Standard for Information Interchange) and EBCDIC (for Extended Binary-Coded-Decimal Interchange Code). EBCDIC is used primarily on large IBM computers. ASCII is used by most other computers. Its character representations are given in Exhibit H.1.

Exhibit H.1 ASCII CODE

DECIMAL	OCTAL	HEXADECIMAL	BINARY	CHARACTER	NOTE
0	000	00	0000000	NUL	null
1	001	01	0000001	SOH	
2	002	02	0000010	STX	
3	003	03	0000011	ETX	
4	004	04	0000100	EOT	
5	005	05	0000101	ENQ	
6	006	06	0000110	ACK	
7	007	07	0000111	BEL	Produces beep or bell
8	010	08	0001000	BS	on terminals
9	011	09	0001001	HT	Backspace (\b)
10	012	0A	0001010	LF	Horizontal tab (\t)
11	013	0B	0001011	VT	Line feed (\n)
12	014	0C	0001100	FF	Vertical tab
13	015	0D	0001101	CR	Form feed (\f)
14	016	0E	0001110	SO	Carriage return (\r)
15	017	0F	0001111	SI	
16	020	10	0010000	DLE	
17	021	11	0010001	DC1	
18	022	12	0010010	DC2	
19	023	13	0010011	DC3	
20	024	14	0010100	DC4	
21	025	15	0010101	NAK	
22	026	16	0010110	SYN	
23	027	17	0010111	ETB	
24	030	18	0011000	CAN	
25	031	19	0011001	EM	
26	032	1A	0011010	SUB	
27	033	1B	0011011	ESC	
28	034	1C	0011100	FS	Escape

Exhibit H.1 ASCII CODE (Continued)

DECIMAL	OCTAL	HEXADECIMAL	BINARY	CHARACTER	NOTE
29	035	1D	0011101	GS	
30	036	1E	0011110	RS	
31	037	1F	0011111	VS	
32	040	20	0100000	SP	
33	041	21	0100001	!	Space
34	042	22	0100010	"	
35	043	23	0100011	#	
36	044	24	0100100	$	
37	045	25	0100101	%	
38	046	26	0100110	&	
39	047	27	0100111	'	
40	050	28	0101000	(	Single quote
41	051	29	0101001	)	
42	052	2A	0101010	*	
43	053	2B	0101011	+	
44	054	2C	0101100	,	
45	055	2D	0101101	-	Comma
46	056	2E	0101110	.	Hyphen
47	057	2F	0101111	/	Period
48	060	30	0110000	0	
49	061	31	0110001	1	
50	062	32	0110010	2	
51	063	33	0110011	3	
52	064	34	0110100	4	
53	065	35	0110101	5	
54	066	36	0110110	6	
55	067	37	0110111	7	
56	070	38	0111000	8	
57	071	39	0111001	9	
58	072	3A	0111010	:	
59	073	3B	0111011	;	Colon
60	074	3C	0111100	<	Semicolon
61	075	3D	0111101	=	
62	076	3E	0111110	>	
63	077	3F	0111111	?	
64	100	40	1000000	@	
65	101	41	1000001	A	
66	102	42	1000010	B	
67	103	43	1000011	C	
68	104	44	1000100	D	
69	105	45	1000101	E	
70	106	46	1000110	F	
71	107	47	1000111	G	

Exhibit H.1 ASCII CODE (Continued)

DECIMAL	OCTAL	HEXADECIMAL	BINARY	CHARACTER	NOTE
72	110	48	1001000	H	
73	111	49	1001001	I	
74	112	4A	1001010	J	
75	113	4B	1001011	K	
76	114	4C	1001100	L	
77	115	4D	1001101	M	
78	116	4E	1001110	N	
79	117	4F	1001111	O	
80	120	50	1010000	P	
81	121	51	1010001	Q	
82	122	52	1010010	R	
83	123	53	1010011	S	
84	124	54	1010100	T	
85	125	55	1010101	U	
86	126	56	1010110	V	
87	127	57	1010111	W	
88	130	58	1011000	X	
89	131	59	1011001	Y	
90	132	5A	1011010	Z	
91	133	5B	1011011	[	
92	134	5C	1011100	\	
93	135	5D	1011101	]	
94	136	5E	1011110	∧	
95	137	5F	1011111	_	Underline
96	140	60	1100000	'	Back quote
97	141	61	1100001	a	
98	142	62	1100010	b	
99	143	63	1100011	c	
100	144	64	1100100	d	
101	145	65	1100101	e	
102	146	66	1100110	f	
103	147	67	1100111	g	
104	150	68	1101000	h	
105	151	69	1101001	i	
106	152	6A	1101010	j	
107	153	6B	1101011	k	
108	154	6C	1101100	l	
109	155	6D	1101101	m	
110	156	6E	1101110	n	
111	157	6F	1101111	o	
112	160	70	1110000	p	
113	161	71	1110001	q	
114	162	72	1110010	r	

Exhibit H.1 ASCII CODE (Continued)

DECIMAL	OCTAL	HEXADECIMAL	BINARY	CHARACTER	NOTE
115	163	73	1110011	s	
116	164	74	1110100	t	
117	165	75	1110101	u	
118	166	76	1110110	v	
119	167	77	1110111	w	
120	170	78	1111000	x	
121	171	79	1111001	y	
122	172	7A	1111010	z	
123	173	7B	1111011	{	
124	174	7C	1111100	|	
125	175	7D	1111101	}	
126	176	7E	1111110	~	
127	177	7F	1111111	(DEL)	Rubout

Storage of numbers

The numbering of bits within a byte varies from computer to computer. On some machines, the leftmost bit is named bit 0 and the rightmost is bit 7. On other machines the leftmost bit is called bit 7 and the rightmost is bit 0.

The order of storage of multi-byte numbers such as two-byte integers also varies. On some systems the more significant byte is first. A integer would be stored in the same order that it appears written. On other machines, the more significant byte is second. This is typically found on 8-bit microprocessors.

Floating point numbers

The representation for floating point numbers varies considerably from computer to computer. Some computers have hardware that performs floating point operations. In others, these operations are performed by subroutines supplied with the compiler. A floating point number is typically represented by four bytes. The first byte contains the exponent (power of 2) and the other three bytes contain the mantissa (or digit part). For example, the decimal number .125 is equal to 1 times 2 raised to the -3 power. This might be represented as[3]:

$2** - 3$ times 1

or:

First byte (exponent)		Next three bytes (mantissa)	
Sign bit	*Value*	*Sign bit*	*Value*
1	3	0	1

or:

10000011   00000000   00000000   00000001

The three mantissa bytes of the floating point number allow it to contain numbers with up to six decimal digits of precision. The double length float number is typically 8 bytes long and has a 7-byte mantissa, which can hold up to 16 decimal digits of precision.

When a floating point number is converted to an integer, the fractional part (anything less than 1) is either thrown away (truncated) or rounded off (used to increment the integer by one if it is greater than .5).

Operators

There are three types of operators commonly found in languages. These are unary, binary, and tertiary. A unary operator acts only on a single variable or value. The most typical is the minus sign (e.g., -5, $-x$). A binary operator requires two operands. In the usual notation (or infix, as it is technically called), the operands appear on either side of the operator (e.g., $5+3$, x/y). Tertiary operators require three operands. The only example in C of a tertiary operator is the conditional operator (?:), which requires a test operand and two result operands.

Footnotes

1. These are the values for computers that use two's complement form for negative numbers. Other common forms (sign magnitude and one's complement) have limits of -127 to $+127$ for 8 bits and $-32,767$ to $+32,767$ for 16 bits. Consult an introductory book on computers for more information on these forms. 2. For more information on octal and hexidecimal number systems, consult an introductory book on computers. 3. Floating point number representation is much more complex than this. Consult an introductory book on computers for more information.

APPENDIX I   FOR BASIC PROGRAMMERS

There are a few concepts of compiled higher level languages with which programmers who know only interpreted BASIC may not be familiar. These include the declaration of variables, subroutine parameters, and main programs. In addition, the concept of variable initialization is somewhat different.

DECLARATIONS

Simple variables in BASIC are declared by implication. The appearance of a character string that is not a keyword is assumed by BASIC to be the name of a variable. The interpreter then sets aside storage space for that variable. Though some languages use this same approach, others make it mandatory that a variable be declared before it is used. These declarations make the interpretation of the program by the compiler easier. They also cut down the possibility of error when entering the program because a misspelled variable name is easier to detect.

BASIC's requirement that arrays with more than 11 elements be declared in a DIM statement acts in a similar manner to this manadatory declaration.

BASIC variables are commonly initialized using combinations of READ and DATA statements. For example:

READ A, B% ,C$

. . .

DATA 32.5,89,"A"

sets the values of A, B% and C$ to 32.5, 89, and "A". The two statements do not need to be located next to each other in the program listing. The initialization of variables in C at the time of declaration keeps the appearance of the values close to the variables. A corresponding set of statements would be:

```
float a=32.5;
int b=89;
char c='A';
```

SUBPROGRAM PARAMETERS

In BASIC, all variables are global. This is, in the entire program, any variable that has the same name refers to the same variable. When a GOSUB is performed, the lines of code in the subroutine reference a variable by the same name by which it is called in the entire program. There are no variables "local" to a subroutine. The values of variables needed by a subroutine must be set up before the GOSUB is executed. For example:

```
20 B=7
30 GOSUB 100
40 PRINT C

    . . .
100 C=2*B
110 RETURN
```

The subroutine at line 100 computes twice the value of B and puts it into C.

With a DEF FN, the value that is passed to a function does not need to be "set up". For example:

```
10 DEF FNP(X) = 2*X

    . . .
100 C=FNP(7)
110 PRINT C
```

X is a formal parameter. It receives the value of 7 when the function is called. This value is used wherever X appears in the function definition.

A function in compiled languages operates as a combination of a DEF FN and a GOSUB. It is a multi-line routine that receives values for its formal parameters and returns a value.

RUN

In order to execute a BASIC program that is entered, typing "RUN" is sufficient. With compiled languages, a series of processes takes place—compilation, assembly, and linking—before a program can be executed (These are described in Appendix J). RUN usually starts the execution of a BASIC program at the first line. With compiled programs, the execution starts with the main program, which is identified in various ways in different languages. In C, the first program to be executed is identified by the name **main**.

APPENDIX J   COMPILATION, LINKING, AND EXECUTION

Unlike programs in purely interpreted languages, such as the BASIC found on many personal computers, a C program requires several steps in order to make it executable by the machine. These steps include preparation of the program, compilation, assembly, and linking. Depending on the compiler and the computer, two or three steps may be combined. The process is shown in Diagram J.1.

PREPARATION

A C program is prepared using a text editor or word processor. By convention, the program file is designated "name.c" where "name" is what the program will be called. The text file is termed the source file or source program. Several files may be used for a single program.

COMPILATION

The compiler takes the source file, interprets it according to the rules of the C langauge, and creates an assembly language file. This file contains the machine language equivalents of the C statements. During the compilation process, the compiler outputs an error message if it finds something in the source file that does not conform to the C language. Usually the assembly language file is called "name.asm" or something similar.

ASSEMBLY

The assembler inputs the assembly language file and outputs a relocatable object code file. This file contains both the actual machine language instructions and information that will be used by the next step, the linker. The relocatable object code file is usually called "name.o".

LINKAGE

The linker examines the relocatable object code file and extracts from library files any routines that are required by the program. It then links all the routines together into an executable code file. This file usually contains only the machine language instructions that will be executed when the program is run. The executable file is usually called "name.exe" or "name.com" or something similar.[1]

Diagram J.1 COMPILATION AND LINKING

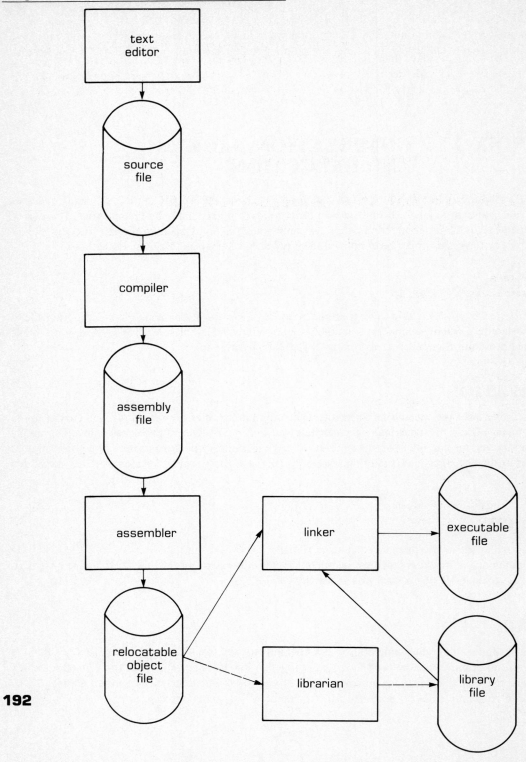

192

LIBRARIAN

If the source file contains routines that are designed to be used by other programs and are not a program in itself, then the librarian rather than the linker, is run. The librarian combines the relocatable object file with other relocatable object files to form a libary file. This library file may then be used during the linkage process. The library file is usually designated "name.lib", where name is what the library is called.[1]

EXECUTION

The executable file may then be run on the computer by typing the name of the file.

OPERATING SYSTEM AND COMPILER DEPENDENCIES

The manual for a particular compiler explains the exact sequence of commands that are required to compile and link a C program. For a typical compiler, these include:

cc name.c	compilation
asm name.asm	assembly
link name.o my.lib system.lib	linkage with two libraries, **my.lib** and **system.lib**
name	executes the program

or to put routines into a library:

c name.c	compilation
asm name.asm	assembly
lib my.lib name.o	putting the routines into library **my.lib**

Under the UNIX operating system, several of these steps are combined into one. By entering **cc name.c**, the compilation, assembly, and linkage are all performed, and an executable file called "a.out" is created. Typing **a.out** will cause the program to run.

Footnotes

1. Many linkers allow several relocatable object files to be linked together at one time, as well as several library files to be searched for routines.

Index